Constructing
Correctional Facilities

Brookings Dialogues on Public Policy

The presentations and discussions at Brookings conferences and seminars often deserve wide circulation as contributions to public understanding of issues of national importance. The Brookings Dialogues on Public Policy series is intended to make such statements and commentary available to a broad and general audience, usually in summary form. The series supplements the Institution's research publications by reflecting the contrasting, often lively, and sometimes conflicting views of elected and appointed government officials, other leaders in public and private life, and scholars. In keeping with their origin and purpose, the Dialogues are not subjected to the formal review procedures established for the Institution's research publications. Brookings publishes them in the belief that they are worthy of public consideration but does not assume responsibility for their accuracy or objectivity. And, as in all Brookings publications, the judgments, conclusions, and recommendations presented in the Dialogues should not be ascribed to the trustees, officers, or other staff members of the Brookings Institution.

Constructing Correctional Facilities

Is There a Role for the Private Sector?

Papers by JAMES K. STEWART

RICHARD P. SEITER

RICHARD L. ENGLER

WILLIAM J. DEASY

CHARLES B. DEWITT & STEVEN D. BINDER

EUGENE C. THOMAS

*presented at a conference at the Brookings Institution,
January 6, 1987*

Edited by JAMES R. SEVICK & WARREN I. CIKINS

THE BROOKINGS INSTITUTION

Washington, D.C.

About Brookings

THE BROOKINGS INSTITUTION is a private nonprofit organization devoted to research, education, and publication in economics, government, foreign policy, and the social sciences generally. Its principal purpose is to bring knowledge to bear on the current and emerging public policy problems facing the American people. In its research, Brookings functions as an independent analyst and critic, committed to publishing its findings for the information of the public. In its conferences and other activities, it serves as a bridge between scholarship and public policy, bringing new knowledge to the attention of decisionmakers and affording scholars a better insight into policy issues. Its activities are carried out through three research programs (Economic Studies, Governmental Studies, Foreign Policy Studies), a Center for Public Policy Education, a Publications Program, and a Social Science Computation Center.

The Institution was incorporated in 1927 to merge the Institute for Government Research, founded in 1916 as the first private organization devoted to public policy issues at the national level; the Institute of Economics, established in 1922 to study economic problems; and the Robert Brookings Graduate School of Economics and Government, organized in 1924 as a pioneering experiment in training for public service. The consolidated institution was named in honor of Robert Somers Brookings (1850–1932), a St. Louis businessman whose leadership shaped the earlier organizations.

Brookings is financed largely by endowment and by the support of philanthropic foundations, corporations, and private individuals. Its funds are devoted to carrying out its own research and educational activities. It also undertakes some unclassified government contract studies, reserving the right to publish its findings.

A Board of Trustees is responsible for general supervision of the Institution, approval of fields of investigation, and safeguarding the independence of the Institution's work. The President is the chief administrative officer, responsible for formulating and coordinating policies, recommending projects, approving publications, and selecting the staff.

Editors' Preface

SEVERE overcrowding in correctional facilities has become a critical issue in the American criminal justice system. The U.S. prison population is more than half a million and growing at unprecedented rates. The increasing number of inmates packed into aging prisons and jails is overburdening physical facilities and straining services. Because of limitations on government budgets in recent years, many jurisdictions have begun to experiment with innovative uses of the private sector.

On January 6, 1987, the Brookings Institution held a seminar to address the issues and problems raised by greater private involvement in prison construction. The seventy-five participants discussed current experiences with private construction; legal and regulatory issues; design, construction, and financing problems; and the future role of private industry in prison construction.

This volume in the Brookings Dialogues on Public Policy series summarizes the results of that conference and presents six of the papers delivered there by federal and state government officials and by private sector experts in prison financing and construction. Jurisdictions interested in potential partnerships with the private sector and businesses planning to offer such services may benefit from the experiences and ideas reported here.

The project greatly benefited from the guidance of a planning committee that included Ray Brown, Charles B. DeWitt, Larry Greenfeld, Hayden Gregory, Jim Hass, Craig Higgins, Wayne Hokom, John Pickett, Alfred Regnery, Judith Schloegel, Donn Smith, Eric Sterling, and Anthony Travisono. Three members of this group—Charles B. DeWitt, Wayne Hokom, and Donn Smith—acted as a steering committee and were especially helpful in the completion of this publication.

The Brookings Institution would like to acknowledge the financial support for this study from the National Institute of Justice of the U.S. Department of Justice. The Morrison Knudsen

Corporation, E. F. Hutton and Company, Inc., Deloitte Haskins and Sells, and Henningson, Durham, and Richardson contributed to the support of the seminar. At Brookings, Donna Marsh and Robert Schley provided organizational assistance.

The views expressed here are those of the authors and should not be ascribed to the organizations whose assistance is acknowledged above or to the trustees, officers, or other staff members of the Brookings Institution.

James R. Sevick
Warren I. Cikins

June 1987
Washington, D.C.

Contents

Introduction

JAMES R. SEVICK

ORDINARILY, a construction boom is a welcome sign for the nation. Construction means more jobs, more homes and office space, and a quickening of the economy. However, the United States, is now in the middle of a construction boom that is being greeted with little enthusiasm. It is a boom in the building of prisons and jails.

The nation is building new correctional institutions in record numbers. In 1987, the federal government will spend more than $150 million on new prison construction. But the biggest builders are the states, which are expected to spend about $3 billion this year for new prison beds. In comparison, as recently as 1981 the total expenditure on prisons was $156 million.[1]

The correctional construction boom comes at a time when state and local governments can hardly afford the cost. States already pay $8 billion each year just to operate existing prisons. New tax laws, debt ceilings, and "voters' revolts" prevent new expenditures in many jurisdictions.

As a result, many jurisdictions have begun to examine new directions for ways to finance, design, and build correctional facilities. Inevitably, that examination has included a study of the private sector. Of course, government has almost always turned to private business for contracts on construction projects. Architectural firms, construction companies, and parts suppliers and manufacturers have routinely been involved in correctional construction. But many jurisdictions have given private firms unprecedented involvement in the planning and construction process in order to meet quickly the demand for new federal and state prison and local jail beds.

The problem of overcrowding

Indeed, demand is far outstripping supply. In the federal prison system alone, the population has doubled, to 41,000, since 1980. It will increase to 67,000 by 1993. State systems are swamped with even more offenders. According to statistics from the

1. *U.S. News and World Report,* February 2, 1987, p. 32.

1

National Institute of Justice (NIJ), at the end of 1985, 503,601 people were in prison. In 1980 the prison population was less than 330,000. There is no indication that this dramatic increase will slow down. In fact, with tougher laws and longer sentences becoming common, the rate of increase may well accelerate. Each week, NIJ estimates, America needs 400 new jail beds and 800 prison beds to keep up with the expanding population.

Because of the population increase, the existing stock of prison beds has been overwhelmed. Every state's correctional system is operating with far more inmates than the number of prison beds available. Nationwide, prisons are at 115 percent of total rated capacity. The situation is so bad that courts have ruled that prison overcrowding is a form of cruel and unusual punishment prohibited by the Bill of Rights. Today, thirty-four states are under court order to alleviate overcrowding.

The need for beds is not simply a result of too many prisoners. The physical plant of the U.S. correctional system is old and getting older. Among our 750 prisons and 3,500 jails, many cells do not meet minimum national standards for space, living conditions, and inmate activities. Of course, overcrowding not only puts stress on the inmates, but also further limits their participation in the programs that many see as important in their rehabilitation. Overcrowding also causes mixing of minor offenders with hard-core criminals, leading to "schools for crime" for which the American correctional system has often been criticized.

Types of private involvement

In recent years, limitations on government budgets have held down prison and jail construction, bringing a dangerous level of overcrowding in many jurisdictions. However, several jurisdictions have experimented in the innovative use of the private sector in the financing and construction of correctional facilities. Some have been so novel and unprecedented that they give new proof for the old cliché that necessity is the mother of invention.

Private involvement in corrections can be divided into three types. First is the financing and construction of prisons. Because of debt limits and the need for votes on bond offerings, jurisdictions have had great difficulty in using conventional financing methods for construction. Private investors have engaged in a variety of lease and lease-purchase arrangements to bypass traditional financing. In these arrangements, the private firm actually owns the facility and leases it to the jurisdiction much the same as if it were an office building. As a result, the jurisdiction can obtain needed bed space without a bond vote or an amendment of debt limits.

In the area of construction, many states have experimented with various types of "construction management" packages, in which a general contractor is hired to oversee all aspects of prison construction. As a result, the jurisdiction, which probably has little experience in large-scale facility construction, can buy the experience of private experts. Moreover, the contractor can obtain the myriad of suppliers and construction services without lengthy public procurement processes. The result is a facility that can be built less expensively, better, and more quickly than is possible through public processes.

The second area of private involvement is in prison industry. Although in its infancy, criminal justice experts place high hopes on this effort, which would install privately owned manufacturing and service industries inside prison walls. The prisoners not only learn good work habits and get job experience; from their salaries they pay taxes, room and board, restitution to victims, and support for their families.

The third area of privatization is the most controversial: management of the facility by a private contractor. Though common in juvenile programs and half-way houses, private management of prisons is a topic fraught with as-yet unresolved legal, managerial, and philosophical questions.

This volume deals *only* with the first area of private involvement, the financing and construction of prisons.

The seminar on constructing corrections facilities

The issue of prison construction is one that will be current for at least another decade. Almost all states, as well as many counties, will face the need for prison or jail construction during that time. All will have difficulty paying for the facilities. It is the area in which private enterprise has played the greatest role, a role which may grow in the coming decade.

For several years the Brookings Institution has conducted national issues forums whose findings have occasionally been summarized in Brookings Dialogues on Public Policy. In these forums, leading members of business, government, and academia join together in discussing critical issues of the day.

The problem of prison construction certainly qualifies as a critical concern, so on January 6, 1987, the Brookings Institution sponsored a "Seminar on Constructing Corrections Facilities: Meeting the Need." The meeting was attended by about seventy-five leaders in the area of corrections. Speakers represented not only criminal justice professionals at the federal, state, and local levels, but also representatives of the private sector who have experience in the area of prison construction.

The purpose of the seminar was to focus on "the shortage of corrections facilities and examine ways of meeting that shortage. It is hoped that, by identifying benefits and costs, successes and failures, and effective and ineffective blueprints, a contribution can be made to meeting an accepted public need."

Speakers at the seminar addressed four general topics related to the involvement of private firms in corrections: current corrections experience; the legal and procurement regulation difficulties; design, construction, and financing problems; and "the road ahead."

This volume summarizes the proceedings of that seminar. It includes six papers particularly useful for policymakers interested in exploring the use of the private sector in prison construction. Overall, the volume intends to give policymakers an understanding of the benefits and pitfalls of the "privatization" of correctional construction. Though discussions at the seminar ranged over many issues involving the private sector and corrections, the focus here is on private construction and financing specifically. The discussion is summarized below, along with the conclusions that emerged.

Overview   The first panel of the seminar presented an overview of activities in correctional construction at the federal, state, and local levels. Norman A. Carlson, director of the Federal Bureau of Prisons, has headed the U.S. effort in prison construction. The Bureau of Prisons has employed three different means to respond to the doubling of its offender population, while still keeping costs to a minimum. First, it has concentrated on the acquisition of existing facilities, which greatly decreases the initial cost of construction. In recent years, the bureau has bought and renovated a decommissioned U.S. Air Force base, a former Jesuit seminary, and a state mental hospital. It is now negotiating the acquisition of a women's college campus. These structures are adaptable for minimium- and medium-security prisons.

The bureau also has added units to existing institutions. By adding a dormitory on an existing site, there is no need to build a new "core facility," that is, the sewer system, heat and power generation plants, and food, recreation, and other service systems.

The construction of new facilities is the third option. As in any prison construction endeavor, the selection of a site is a major problem. The Bureau of Prisons has a "marketing" section, which tours potential sites and educates the leaders and the public about the advantages of a prison. It employs a lot of workers, both during construction and operation. Unlike other industries, the prison will not move to a foreign country or go bankrupt.

The bureau constantly emphasizes two other factors in its construction program. First, it is very aware of the life-cycle costs of an institution and designs its facilities to minimize the use of guard stations and areas requiring high staffing levels. Electronic monitoring is used extensively. Second, the federal system utilizes a classification system in building prisons. A strong classification system for prisoners can hold down costs by clarifying the security levels needed for the inmate population and matching beds to inmates. Minimum security beds can cost one-fifth as much as maximum security beds. The U.S. Penitentiary at Marion, Illinois, is the federal system's ultimate maximum security prison, where "violent predators" are housed. Through classification techniques, the bureau is able to limit the population at Marion to 350, out of the total federal population of 41,000.

The final factor in the success of the federal system is its highly qualified and trained staff. Austin McCormick, a prison warden, wrote a classic book on corrections entitled *The Old Red Barn*. The title reflects the thesis of the book: with a well-trained staff, a prison can be operated in any facility, even an old red barn.

Anthony Travisono, executive director of the American Corrections Association (ACA), reemphasized the critical importance of classification and staff training in holding down prison costs. He also addressed the need for long-term planning for correctional systems. In the 1970s, several states closed down institutions or halted construction activities because of political pressures, even though it was clear that the need for beds would increase.

Legal and regulatory constraints

In the second panel, the seminar addressed the problems related to current legal and regulatory constraints on the use of the private sector in corrections. The construction of a prison is a unique activity in government operations, and many regulations governing their construction were written for vastly different undertakings. As a result, the use of the private sector in many jurisdictions may be illegal. In other cases, policymakers have been able to make creative use of existing regulations to involve the private sector.

H. E. Davis, Jr., the purchasing agent for the county of Los Angeles, has been closely involved in the expansion of L.A. County's prison facilities, which currently hold more than 17,000 inmates in rated capacity for 12,000. As the county's purchasing agent, he has broad powers to construct new buildings. Whoever the purchasing agent in a jurisdiction, that person should be able to conduct procurement activities independently, without interference from the legislative body, be it a city council or a state legislature. The close participation in a procurement by a legislative body greatly slows the procurement activity. Furthermore, their participation can inject political factors into siting and construction decisions.

Siting is always a major problem in correctional construction, and its political repercussions are such that it will strongly influence the rest of the project. Not surprisingly, prison sites are often chosen in the most sparsely populated areas. This, of course, is not conducive for inmate programs and preservation of prison family ties.

The construction management team

Particularly at the county level, there is little institutional experience on how to build a prison or jail. As a result, many jurisdictions hire a construction manager to oversee all aspects of the project. The construction manager is somewhat akin to the general contractor in private construction. He has wide authority to select subcontractors for the design and construction of the new facility. This usually leads to a more professionally run project, with lower costs and faster construction schedules than a publicly managed effort.

But despite the utility of the project management model, intensive involvement will still be required from the jurisdiction. One should add representatives to the project team from all agencies directly or indirectly related to the construction. Not only the police department, but also agencies like the county or city engineer, the building department, the fire department, and the purchasing office should be represented. The jurisdiction's chief administrative officer, such as the city manager, should also participate.

It is important to appoint the architect to the project team at the earliest stage. In a procurement the size of a jail or prison, there are many questions and problems that only the participation of the architect can resolve.

The personality of the project administrator or director also has great bearing on the success of the project. That person must be able to forge a clear direction among the six or seven or more different perspectives and opinions that will be represented on the project team.

Political will

Joseph diGenova, U.S. attorney for the District of Columbia, touched on the need for strong political will in bringing about completion of a prison construction project. The District currently has a court order on every correctional institution in its jurisdiction. Something had to be done to alleviate crowding.

The crowding did not develop because of tough sentencing alone. About 90 percent of District inmates are recidivists. Instead, it developed from poor planning—a failure to recognize that drug convictions would swell the imprisoned population, despite stable crime rates in other areas.

The decision to build or not to build is simply a decision about the level of risk reduction that society desires. The fewer offenders incarcerated, the greater the risk that crime rates will increase. However, it is difficult for politicians to recognize this. It is up to criminal justice professionals—police, prosecutors, and correctional officials—to educate politicians and the public about the trade-offs between prison costs and crime rates. Only by honestly assessing needs, and conveying those needs to the public, can this country reduce the overcrowding problem through well-planned construction programs.

Limits on the private sector

Frank Panarisi, a director for the consulting firm of Deloitte, Haskins, & Sells, discussed legal problems connected with the use of private firms in correctional construction. These are largely involved with current procurement regulations that inhibit the free use of private firms. Many jurisdictions have limitations on the size of procurements that can be awarded without competition. The new techniques in construction management, such as the project management model, usually require the early selection of a general contractor; this step may be prohibited by regulation. Other procurement regulations require that public land be leased or sold to the highest bidder. These regulations may affect lease-purchase arrangements and similar innovative financing methods. General questions and legal requirements about debt limits and general obligation bonds must always be carefully studied when considering private financing.

Nevertheless, many jurisdictions have creatively employed legislation to overcome impediments to privatization. For example, the state of California faced regulations that required local jurisdictions to go through a competitive bidding process on jail construction. However, in 1986 legislation was passed permitting any sheriff under court order to alleviate jail crowding, or any county more than 20 percent over its rated jail capacity, to streamline the bidding process. The basis of the legislation was that crowding was a danger to health and public safety. It is applicable to most of the counties in California.

Other jurisdictions have circumvented competitive bid regulations by leasing public land to a development company, which then builds a jail on the land and in turn leases the facility back to the county.

The case against private management

Ira Robbins, professor of law at American University, presented several arguments against the use of private industry in corrections. Though most of the opposition to privatization is in the area of private facility management, the philosophical, legal, and moral points have implications for private construction issues as well.

Though many extol the speed with which the private sector can act, critics of privatization consider swiftness a serious drawback. In bureaucracy, they say, the pace is slow, but there is the guarantee that all components of the community have their say. Public hearings and procurement procedures take time, but they are more likely to avoid colossal errors of judgment to which the headlong activity of the private sector is subject.

Of particular concern to opponents of private construction is their belief that lease-purchase financing may be illegal because it tries to circumvent the requirement in many jurisdictions that the public vote on all major capital expenditures. The privatization of construction through lease arrangements, critics say, is a device that deprives the public of its right to vote "no" to prison construction. It circumvents democracy.

A congressional view

An address by Representative Bill McCollum (R–Fla.) presented a congressional view on the privatization of corrections. A serious problem in criminal justice is the lack of appreciation among policymakers of the systemic nature of criminal justice. This could be clearly seen in the passage of the Federal Anti-drug Abuse Act of 1986. In the debate about that act, many in Congress realized that the implication of mandatory prison terms for drug dealers was a vast increase in the size of the prison population. Acordingly, there was a request to build nine new medium-security federal prisons, which would have accomodated the increased arrest rate and longer sentences. The drug bill passed, but Congress approved the construction of only two new prisons.

Nevertheless, the experience in Congress did open many legislators' eyes to the severely overcrowded conditions in the prisons. As a result, Congress is expected to approve more funds for construction this year. This situation underlines the need for constant education of the public and the policymakers about the needs of the criminal justice system.

Advantages of innovative construction management

Gerard Frey is planning coordinator for the Department of Corrections and Human Services in Missouri. That state, like many others, has built several facilities in the last few years. Most of these projects used traditional planning and procurement methods. As a result, most were late and over budget. Furthermore, the cost overruns resulted in cutting features from the design. Bedspace was cut, industry space was curtailed, and building materials were cheapened. In the end, the state got facilities that did not meet its plans and were still too expensive and too slow in construction.

Missouri switched to a lease-purchase arrangement for its most recent project, a 500-bed maximum-security facility. For this effort, it hired an architectural firm to write the request for proposals (RFP), which was extremely detailed. Nearly $2 million were spent in the design of the facility. The resulting RFP was put out to bid, and eight firms submitted proposals. Many entered into joint ventures with communities in Missouri, which were anxious to obtain the new facility. The firm that wrote the RFP also evaluated the proposals.

The winning city was Potosi. The builder assumes all the costs until the building is brought on line, so he has a stong incentive to complete it on time. The price of the project is fixed: $4.6 million each year for the next thirty years. Since Missouri, like most states, can only contract for periods of one year, the builder is also accepting a large risk in assuming that it will be leased for the full thirty-year period. However, as a result, he is being extremely responsive to the state's needs. The state knows it is getting exactly what it pays for.

The road ahead

The final panel of the seminar addressed the future of private involvement in correctional construction. Commissioner Helen G. Corrothers, a member of the U.S. Sentencing Commission, reported on the status of the commission and how its findings were expected to influence the prison population. The commission, established through the Comprehensive Crime Control Act of 1984, received a difficult mandate from Congress. The commission is to review federal sentencing policies and practices and develop new guidelines for sentencing. The guidelines are to avoid unwarranted disparities in sentencing and also take into account the four purposes of incarceration: just punishment for offenders; the societal need for deterrence of future crime; the need for incapacitation of career criminals; and the rehabilitation of offenders. Finally, it is to develop its recommendations in such a way as to minimize the likelihood that the federal population will exceed the capacity of the federal prison system.

Three factors will affect the findings of the commission and will result in a tendency toward higher populations. First, the legislation requires that drug dealers and repeat offenders receive "substantial prison terms," and mandatory sentencing is required in many cases. Furthermore, sentences are to reflect the seriousness of the crime. Finally, the Anti-drug Abuse Act of 1986 also stipulates sentences for a variety of drug offenders.

Although these factors will pressure the federal system to build more beds, there are also strong financial pressures for finding alternatives to incarceration. Principal among these pressures are that a new prison cell costs between $25,000 and $125,000 to build and that it costs $7,000 to $30,000 each year to keep an inmate in prison. But financial pressures alone cannot so limit the incarcerated population as to cause disregard for the aspect of the just sentence for offenders. Nor should disrespect for the law and the courts be promoted.

Third, recent statistics show that one white male in thirty-five is either incarcerated or under some form of correctional supervision. These figures suggest that jail and prison crowding will continue to be issues until there is a fundamental change in behavior in our society.

Finally, Arnold Burns, U.S. deputy attorney general, discussed the increased role of public-private partnerships throughout society and urged that public officials keep an open mind toward work with the private sector. In the last few years, business has become involved with many facets of government that had previously been considered havens of the public sector. This has resulted not simply because it is the policy of the current administration to increase the role of the private sector in government, but because of the realization at the federal, state, and local levels that government has a lot to learn from business. In many cases, government cannot act at all without the participation of the private sector. Limitations on taxation and spending at every level of government has left legislators and administrators with the choice of either widening the role of the private sector or facing a loss of services to the public.

The current overcrowding crisis is the most difficult problem the criminal justice system has had to deal with in a long time. According to Burns, the system has to accept useful ideas and innovations, wherever they come from. Now is not the time to bicker about turf questions or worry about whether an innovation comes from the public or the private sector.

Business has already offered a number of innovations in the field of corrections. New financing methods and new construction and design techniques clearly are important advancements. But more subtle domains are also affected. Improvements in management, information processing, training, and other areas of corrections also had their beginnings in private business.

The key to overcoming the prison population crisis lies in partnership and cooperation. According to Burns, "Only by working together, hand in hand, can we see our way through the current overpopulation crisis."

Conclusions

Private-sector participation in corrections has been such a volatile issue that, even among correctional professionals, there is a wide divergence of opinion about its utility, legal standing, and political, moral, and philosophical worth. Even less agreement could be expected among the variety of political leaders, criminal justice leaders, and business executives who participated in the seminar.

Nevertheless, several areas of agreement did emerge from the discussion. The predominant view among all groups is that prison and jail overcrowding has become a problem of national concern. The stress on the correctional system is already alarming, and all projections agree that the problem will be much worse in five years.

Stemming from that fact is the general conclusion that, to alleviate overcrowding, the construction of new prisons and jails is an absolute necessity, not only for the federal and state systems, but for many counties and municipalities as well. This is not to say that additional bedspace is the only solution. Many experts are confident that alternative programs for new and nonviolent offenders are more likely to lead to rehabilitation than incarceration. Others hope that new technologies, such as house arrest through electronic monitoring, can ease the crowding problem. But even if these strategies are successful, there is still a need to build more prison beds and to renovate the aging physical plant of existing facilities.

Many panelists concluded that overcrowding will continue to be a problem as long as the judiciary continues to send mixed signals about corrections. The judiciary has placed the correctional system in jeopardy by pursuing *incarceration policies* that send more offenders to prison than before, while at the same time demanding by court order that the institutions prevent overcrowding. This problem is a systemic one. The criminal justice system, from police through corrections, must be better educated about the effects of each component of the system on "downstream" activities. The more offenders police arrest, the more prosecutors prosecute, and the more judges sentence, the more overcrowding occurs in prison. As the last in line, corrections has the choice of overcrowding or releasing criminals into the community.

Education is also needed for the public. In the final analysis, overcrowding has resulted from the contradictory desires of the public. On the one hand, public opinion has demanded that society get tough on crime. This has encouraged strict enforcement, mandatory sentencing, and stiffer penalties. At the same time, the public, through its legislatures as well as direct voting on bond proposals, has stifled the construction of new facilities to house the larger populations.

Most of the seminar participants agreed that major changes in procurement procedures were necessary in many jurisdictions. Modern construction management techniques like the use of a construction manager, a general contractor, or a design-build consortium have long been used in private construction. These techniques have saved time and money and improved the quality of the facilities, both in their construction and in their use by the corrections departments.

The employment of new construction techniques has also benefited corrections by greater attention to the facility's design. Proper design improves facilities in two ways. First, it improves the likelihood that the institution will meet the needs of the corrections department in terms of security levels, staffing levels, programming, and industries. Second, design controls life-cycle costs. Savings in staffing that result from good design dwarf the additional costs required to plan the facility.

Greater planning in all phases of design and construction was also a common theme at the seminar. In traditional procurement and financing procedures, the players have not sufficiently coordinated their activities to bring about a result satisfying to all. Those players include not only members of the corrections department but also the legislative body and executive, the procurement agency, the financing and revenue agencies, engineers, and numerous other authorities. Whether using traditional or private sector mechanisms, the utmost coordination of players, usually through a project team, is an absolute necessity.

Private Industry and Corrections

JAMES K. STEWART

MEETING the need for more correctional facilities is one of the highest priorities in the U.S. criminal justice system. That system is in deep trouble. Between 1978 and 1985, the shortfall of prison beds in the United States rose by more than 100 percent. By 1985, 55,000 more people were in prison than U.S. correctional institutions were designed to hold. But the issue is more than just numbers. The issue is more than the cost of the lawsuits, liability awards, and court orders resulting from overcrowding. It is more than the negative effects of crowding on inmates, correctional staff, and correctional programs. The imperative to expand correctional capacity in this country even goes beyond concerns about financing and beyond fears that correctional policy will be reduced to mere "warehousing" of offenders.

The need for more facilities is grounded in the primary responsibility of the U.S. criminal justice system—to ensure the public safety. The current insufficiency in prison and jail space adds impetus, and this insufficiency distorts all other segments of the criminal justice system.

Fear of crime and victimization remain critical public concerns, and legitimately so. One out of four American families were victims of crime last year. The rates at which career offenders commit crimes are appallingly high; one offender can commit hundreds of crimes in a single year, particularly when he is using drugs. Increasingly, society recognizes that the incarceration of career criminals is essential to ensure the public safety.

Diversion   Yet a recent nationwide survey of criminal justice professionals by the National Institute of Justice (NIJ) found that the most critical issue facing state and local criminal justice systems is prison and jail crowding.[1] Corrections officials, police, prosecutors, and judges agree that sufficient prison space was simply not available.

James K. Stewart is the director of the National Institute of Justice, U.S. Department of Justice.

1. Stephen Gettinger, *Assessing Criminal Justice Needs*, National Institute of Justice (NIJ), Research in Brief (Washington, D.C.: NIJ, 1984).

13

Each group expressed frustration that crowding inhibits its ability to do its job.

Police complain of the "revolving door" syndrome. For example, they invest extensive planning, resources, and overtime manpower for major sweeps, such as Operation Pressure Point in New York City. Through these sweeps, police arrest large numbers of people who possess large quantities of narcotics. Yet those offenders are often back on the street hours after arrest. Even when they are convicted, they frequently receive probation, because the jail is too crowded to accept any but the most violent, high-risk offenders.

So at the "front end" of the criminal justice system, overcrowding results in diversion of offenders from the correctional system.

Sentencing discounts

Perhaps the most troubling aspect of crowding is that the lack of capacity forces deep sentencing discounts. Compare, for example, the armed robbers convicted in federal courts in 1961 with those convicted in 1985. Formal time sentenced increased from an average of 127 months in 1961 to 155 months in 1985. This increase indicates that armed robbery is increasingly considered a serious crime, to be punished with increasingly serious penalties. Although sentences rose, time served decreased from fifty-seven months to forty-four months in 1985.

There is no "truth in sentencing," and the evidence is even more dramatic for drug offenses. In the federal system, 83 percent of drug offenders went to prison in 1961, but only 74 percent received prison terms in 1985. The average sentence also decreased from seventy-four months to sixty-five. But the crucial indicator is the time served. This period decreased from thirty-nine months in 1961 to nineteen months—less than 30 percent of time sentenced—in 1985. That is a real discount. A 70 percent reduction is more than anyone will get in most after-Christmas sales. One questions whether the American people really want to put fire-sale discounts on justice.

Alternatives to incarceration

One consequence of crowding, then, is the early release of prisoners—more than 18,000 in 1985 alone. Many of those released early will commit new crimes that their incarceration might have prevented. Some serious offenders never go to prison at all. Clearly this situation poses a serious threat to public safety.

According to one of NIJ's studies, when convicted felons in California were given probation instead of prison terms, two-thirds were rearrested while still under supervision.[2] These crimes, and many others that went undetected, would not have happened, categorically would not have happened, had space been available to incarcerate the offenders. And crime is more than just a statistic. For each crime committed, there are victims who suffer financial loss, personal harm, and psychological trauma.

The idea of house arrest has never been a viable alternative to incarceration because we cannot be certain that the arrestee is staying at home, and probation departments do not have enough staff to supervise house arrestees. Some new technologies hold the promise for closer supervision for some of the 1.9 million people, mostly felons, who are currently on probation. Electronic monitoring devices, for example, may give the courts the ability to place an offender under house arrest and to monitor that arrest through telemetry. An arrestee who leaves his or her house will thus trigger an alarm at the police station, or at least cause the transgression to be recorded.

The electronic monitor may give the criminal justice system a new policy option, but it is only a supplement to community probation. It is not a substitute for jail or prison.

The need for additional capacity

For too many years, we have focused on the wrong number in our correctional system. The question about capacity is not whether the number of available cells ought to determine the prison population, or whether the system is too crowded, or whether the prison population should double in five years. Rather, the determination about who belongs in prison should be determined by the number of victims of serious crime. All people guilty of a crime should pay the price for that crime.

The debate in America is no longer about whether we need additional capacity; that decision has already been made. The decision to expand prison beds has been made at the state, federal, and local levels. It is a bipartisan decision that also cuts across socioeconomic boundaries.

The debate now concerns how this expansion can be accomplished efficiently and economically, how many new beds are needed, how the facilities should be designed, and who ought to manage them. In state legislatures and in local communities, the public increasingly supports expanding facilities. California, for example, appropriated $2.1 billion in the past four years to support a correctional construction program.

2. Joan Petersilia, *Probation and Felony Offenders*, NIJ, Research in Brief (Washington, D.C.: NIJ, 1985).

Possibilities for the private sector

The private sector—the driving force in our economy—has come forward with some promising, innovative approaches to prison construction. New private enterprises and public-private partnerships are appearing, many of which offer stimulating ways to review, renew, and improve our corrections system.

The system has suffered from public neglect. Both the private sector and the public sector have neglected it. Only dedicated corrections professionals have staunchly tried to maintain a modern, efficient, and humane prison system, but they have not received sufficient support. Private enterprise and numerous developments in correctional construction can help those professionals who for so many years have done so well by themselves to keep an aging system alive.

These developments have taken many forms. For example, one area in which the National Institute of Justice has undertaken a serious initiative is in the effort to facilitate quick and economical prison construction. A cartoon by Gary Larson epitomizes this effort. In it, a professor is standing in front of a large blackboard filled with equations. The caption reads: "Einstein proves that time equals money."

Many sheriffs and corrections officials are beginning to prove the same thing. They have used advanced designs, progressive construction techniques, and prefabrication methods to reduce dramatically the time, and therefore the cost, of prison construction.

Those in charge of building new facilities must have access to the most progressive and economical construction techniques. As Attorney General Edwin Meese III has said, "There is no reason why a prison facility should cost $100,000 per cell to construct in one area, and $30,000 to $40,000 to construct the same cell someplace else."[3]

Construction bulletins

The NIJ is moving to provide useful information to those jurisdictions that must expand their facilities, appropriate funds, and manage the new institutions. The institute is publishing a series of "Construction Bulletins."[4] Recent bulletins focus on activities in Virginia and California. Both states have used the concept of "construction management," a new approach to

3. Quoted in Charles B. DeWitt, *New Construction Methods for Corrections Facilities*, NIJ, Construction Bulletin Series (Washington, D.C.: NIJ, 1986), p. 3.

4. The series of bulletins and other materials on corrections construction are available from the National Criminal Justice Reference Service, Construction Information Exchange, Rockville, Md.

construction that emphasizes planning and centralization of decisions about construction. Further savings in these facilities were achieved through the use of prefabricated concrete panels.

Another bulletin details the construction of a Florida prison, where concrete cell modules were lifted into place with a tractor crane. Recently, the Federal Bureau of Prisons has also used this innovative method to expand its facility at Oakdale, Louisiana. Another bulletin discusses Ohio's approach to construction and financing. Ohio's Ross Correctional Institution was built using precast concrete panels and components. The savings in this new technique amounted to about $13 million. The cost for each cell was about $40,000, far below the national average.

Ohio is also a pioneer in its financing of prison constructon through lease-purchase arrangements. Instead of using fixed-rate bond issuances, the traditional method for financing, Ohio has used variable-rate financing. These financing methods have saved the state more than $3 million in the first year alone.

In every case, the innovations developed by these states have resulted in great advantages in time and money compared with conventional construction methods.

Directory of corrections construction

The institute has also published a national directory of corrections construction.[5] The directory contains profiles of facilities built or remodeled in this country since 1978, with floor plans and detailed architectural information about each one. This directory will be available to the people who make the decision to build correctional facilities. They will have the chance to review the "state of the art" in correctional construction and to benefit from the experiences of those who have already planned, financed, and built new facilities.

The cover of our directory shows the Federal Correction Institution (FCI) at Phoenix, Arizona. This institution is an excellent example of how time and money can be saved through careful planning. It is, in fact, the feature of an upcoming construction bulletin by Bureau of Prisons Director Norman Carlson. The state of South Carolina acquired the plans of FCI, Phoenix, and recently built one just like it. Time and money were saved because South Carolina learned from the experience of others.

5. National Institute of Justice, *National Directory of Corrections Construction* (Washington, D.C.: Government Printing Office, 1986).

*Construction
information
exchange*

Another part of the NIJ program is the Construction Information Exchange, operated through our National Criminal Justice Reference Service. This information exchange will introduce officials who are about to embark on construction to their counterparts in jurisdictions in which similar projects have been completed. Though these programs focus on construction issues, we must remember that staffing and operations cost much more in the life cycle of an institution. Construction costs make up only 10 percent of the total operating cost over a thirty-year period. Correctional administrators can benefit from the experiences of colleagues who, in the words of one sheriff, have already "survived the ordeal" of planning a new facility.

Financing

The criminal justice system must also be creative in searching for new sources of revenue and developing new sources of financing. Some states, like California and Kentucky, have passed laws to dedicate criminal fines and forfeitures to the financing of correctional facilities. Other jurisdictions are urging new sales taxes or revenues from prison industries. The sale of goods from prison industry is still illegal in many states. Legal prohibitions to income-producing activities hurt the ability of these states to finance construction.

The private sector has become increasingly active in the development of financing packages. Jurisdictions should look at these new opportunities. Lease-purchase agreements, for example, have many advantages over traditional bonds. Companies like Morrison Knudsen and E.F. Hutton have joined with public agencies in partnerships that provide the services necessary to finance, design, and build institutions. In traditional, public sector approaches, each of these phases requires separate, time-consuming periods for contracting.

*Facility
management*

Lease-purchasing arrangements result in nominal private ownership of corrections facilities, but these facilities might otherwise never be built because of difficulties in obtaining public financing. However, this situation does not represent nearly as great a policy shift as would complete private ownership and management.

There are a few such new projects and experiments under way that open a whole new area for private enterprise. The most notable is the private correctional facility in Marion County, Kentucky, which opened last year with a capacity to serve more than 200 minimum-security inmates.

Though contracts for the private operation of halfway houses and work-release programs have long been a feature of many correctional systems, Kentucky is the first state to contract for the private management of a facility that houses a mainstream adult criminal population. Interest in private management of adult correctional facilities has generally been restrained because adult offenders usually present greater problems than do juveniles. Adults have longer terms of confinement, need more elaborate services, and are subject to more stringent security. Kentucky, however, proceeded with the project only after extensive study and analysis. The analysis revealed that the private sector may provide substantially improved service.

A current NIJ study has found that, during 1985, at least eight states were considering private contracting options, but all are approaching the issue cautiously.[6] Most states were considering private management of minimum-security institutions, hoping that the experience might be similar to that of contracting for halfway house operation.

Privately operated facilities have been used quite frequently in juvenile corrections. Although most have been small in size, a major Florida juvenile facility at Ojakobi has recently been transferred to private management. In Colorado, a private 240-bed juvenile facility is scheduled to open soon, and it will receive juvenile offenders from any state in the country.

The NIJ study of private industry in corrections analyzes the issues that states should consider when deciding whether to contract, as well as discussing the administration and evaluation of contract operations.

At the local level, a few jurisdictions in Florida, Tennessee, and Minnesota are experimenting with private jail management. On the other hand, there is growing interest in expanding the use of contracts for specific correctional services. A study by the National Institute of Corrections found that privately provided services, such as medical and food service, were often considered cheaper and more effective than those provided by public agencies.

Private industry programs

The NIJ has also examined how various public-private partnerships can be made more productive. In 1985, the institute published "The Privatization of Corrections," the first comprehensive analysis of the challenges and opportunities in the field. In that year, it also sponsored a three-day forum, "Corrections and the Private

---

6. Joan Mullen and others, *The Privatization of Corrections* (Government Printing Office, 1985).

Sector," which drew nearly 300 state and local corrections administrators, sheriffs, and business representatives. The keynote speaker at the forum was former Chief Justice Warren Burger. He is particularly interested in an area that may hold the greatest potential for corrections: the introduction of the private sector to prison industries. Justice Burger has a deep commitment to the concept of prisons as "factories with fences," as opposed to warehouses with walls.

In early 1986, private sector firms directed about twenty-six different prison industry programs, with a capital investment of about $3.5 million. In these programs, inmates do the work and earn competitive wages in producing goods and services that are often sold on the open market. In terms of gross sales, the most notable prison industry is Best Western's computer reservation system in an Arizona women's institution. In Mississippi, inmates manufacture condensing units for Cool Mist.

The Control Data Corporation also used prison inmates in Minnesota to assemble computer parts. They had to compete with the Asian countries, whose talents and skills in producing electronic goods are legendary. As a result of training, the inmates became highly proficient in assembling disk drives. In fact, the quality and acceptance of their products exceeded that enjoyed by their Asian competitors. Furthermore, the prison work force was always at work. There were no vacations or special holidays to worry about.

Most private prison industries have appeared in the past five years. The income generated by inmate salaries pays taxes, prisoners' room and board, family support, and victims' compensation.

Prison industry may be a big advance in correctional practice. It may turn a liability—idle time in prison—into an asset—productive labor. If we can enable inmates to work at market wages, we can increase their productivity, reduce the cost of prisons, reduce inmate idleness, and give them the skills and experience they need to hold a real, competitive job when they are released. The improved work force can have a reinforcing effect, bringing more private industry into the prisons.

For the first time in American corrections, we can establish programs that truly benefit incarcerated offenders. A myriad of by-products would result; for example, the prisoner's family could visit prison and keep family ties strong, rather than visiting the welfare office to try to survive. If we can get the family to worry about how "Joe" is doing in prison, in his training, and in his job, then we may be able to bond the family more closely, rather than driving it apart.

The authors of "The Privatization of Corrections" strongly recommend the development of industrial prisons, bringing to life Chief Justice Burger's idea of a factory with fences. Such an institution offers the greatest opportunity, perhaps, for private management. The concern for productive work experience in prison, fostered ardently by the chief justice, stimulates the strong interest in this topic today.

The status of private industry in corrections

Many of these new ventures are promising. Private ownership and management of facilities might increase the speed in making facilities operational and improve the flexibility for experimentation without permanent capital investment, as well as increasing economies of scale. However, private ownership faces many challenges: the delegation of the state's authority to incarcerate, the resistance of public employees and employee unions, and legal concerns about contractor liability and potential instability.

Whether private facilities can offer better services at lower costs is still open to question. The limited information now available gives no indication that contractors are taking excess profits, and the correctional agencies involved in private management seem satisfied that their contractors are performing well.

In short, the preliminary report card is good and very promising. However, in preparing for private management, corrections agencies must take extreme care. Contracts and procurement regulations must be comprehensive. Operating guidelines must make clear that correctional standards will be maintained or exceeded.

It is doubtful that the present U.S. system will ever be replaced by "prisons for profit." Nevertheless, the public sector must be open to areas in which the private sector can offer savings, useful alternatives, and efficient methods. As President Ronald Reagan has often asserted, the development of more partnerships between the public and private sectors is crucial to the continued success of our government and our society.

In corrections, the challenge is to use each sector to its best advantage. The discipline and creativity of the private sector can be enormously important in the coming years, particularly as facilities modernize and expand. The corrections system today is a "buyers' market." We have to foresee how that market can best be served. We must keep our minds open so that each sector can make its contribution.

Ohio's Program
for Prison Construction

RICHARD P. SEITER

THE STATE OF Ohio has a success story to tell about prison construction. It is very satisfying that the Brookings Institution and the National Institute of Justice have taken an interest in Ohio's activities as it has endeavored to meet its needs for additional prison space.

The state followed the lead of the Federal Bureau of Prisons in making full use of existing facilities. Five existing state facilities—hospitals and other complexes—have been converted into prisons in the last four years. Existing correctional institutions expanded their capacity; the state converted attics, dug out crawl spaces, and did everything possible to add bed space. Despite these measures, Ohio only has a current capacity of about 13,000, and the current inmate count is 22,000. Clearly, overcrowding is the correctional system's biggest concern.

The rise in prison population

Prison populations consist of two variables: the number of people convicted by the courts and the length of time those people remain in prison. From 1973 to 1983, Ohio saw a tremendous increase in the number of people sent to state prisons. A higher percentage of convicted offenders were being incarcerated, and a smaller percentage were put on probation. In the early 1970s, the correctional system received about 5,000 new prisoners each year; in the mid-1980s, approximately 10,000 people each year go to prison in the state of Ohio. In 1982, the General Assembly passed a "get tough on crime" law, which increased the time that offenders spend in prison by 60 percent.

As a result of these two changes, the state's prison population rose from 16,000 in 1983 to 22,000 in 1987. And those inmates are staying a lot longer. The most conservative projections indicate that Ohio will have nearly 30,000 inmates by the early 1990s.

For Ohio, prison construction is not a panacea for prison overcrowding. Nevertheless, the state's $500 million, 14-institution,

Richard P. Seiter is director of the Ohio Department of Rehabilitation and Corrections.

10,000-bed construction program may at least show us the "light at the end of the tunnel." It may also enable the state to enter the 1990s better prepared to meet the challenge of protecting the public safety.

Many questions must be answered to explain adequately what makes a successful prison construction program. Like a news story, the story of the Ohio program includes aspects of the "who, what, when, where, why, and how" of prison construction. All these aspects are important. Where to build—prison siting— has been an extremely frustrating issue in Ohio. The "who, when, and why" are political questions that will vary from state to state. But the most useful aspects of the Ohio story for other states and localities are the "what and how" of prison construction: what type of facility to build to meet the needs, and how to build, in a cost-effective manner, a new institution that is the best that it can be.

The Ohio story is not an original one. It borrows heavily from the story of the Federal Bureau of Prisons, in what it does and how it does it. Through the leadership of Norman Carlson, the federal prison system has been the standard that the states have looked to as they try to meet prison space problems efficiently and economically.

Similarity of design

The Ohio construction program's first guiding principle has been to create a standard design for prisons. All fourteen new institutions will be fairly similar. They will have small, decentralized, self-contained housing units, surrounded by a tough, sophisticated perimeter fence. This overall principle gives the prison the "best of both worlds": a secure perimeter and a relaxed, tension-free, easy-to-manage environment inside the compound.

Ohio has also borrowed from the federal system in designing institutions based on the concept of unit management: breaking down the prison into small groups of inmates, with more direct involvement by the staff. This concept should create a safer, more humane environment inside.

The fourteen new facilities range in size from 200 to 1,250 beds. Despite the difference in size, the designs are similar. The standard unit is 125 beds, with separate administration, warehouse, and program spaces. The state has endeavored to meet the national standard in corrections of a 500-bed facility. In institutions with more than 500 beds, the compounds are divided into 500-bed components.

Selection of architects

The selection of architects is a critical aspect of the construction program. Ohio has not had as many problems with architects as other states and has been fortunate to have selected firms that can put in place the operational and management philosophies of the Ohio corrections department. The Ohio Division of Public Works—the builders of all public edifices in state government—gives the corrections department a "short list" of architectural firms, but the department may select one firm from that list.

Once we select the architect, we begin a detailed planning process, prior to the design phase, to ensure a speedy design process. As James K. Stewart said, "Time is money." The time taken up by numerous approval meetings, and redesign resulting from poor planning and miscommunication, can be extremely expensive. So the predesign sessions with the architects ensure an understanding of exactly what we want.

We then create a three-person steering committee to provide liaison with the architects. The team represents the department at the architects' working sessions. This liaison gives the architects immediate responses to questions about design.

State corrections systems have suffered from their inability to say, before and during design: "This is how we want to operate the prison. This is what we want to talk to the architects about. These are the things the prison design must encompass. This is how that affects the management and operation of the facility for years to come." The steering committee permits Ohio to give this information to the architects in a precise and consistent manner. Consequently, the needs of corrections professionals can be interpreted in the design phase by the architects. This committee has worked effectively. The state has had good experiences both with large national firms that have already built prisons, as well as with those that have never designed a prison.

Security levels

Another critical aspect of prison construction is the security level of its inmates, which is important not only for the physical design but also for the cost. Costs can vary tremendously from minimum to maximum security. Therefore, the state must have a good classification system. The prison population must be stratified, and the stratification must be used to make projections of future numbers of inmates and their security levels. With these projections, it is possible to predict the number of minimum-, medium-, and maximum-security beds needed in the system.

The cost of overbuilding high-security beds can be dramatic. On the other hand, the state needs some flexibility to adjust to population changes and to revise security levels of some beds.

Project management

The state is also using the construction management approach, at least to some extent. We call it "project management" in Ohio because it does not include the typical fee structure and responsibilities that a construction manager would have in the private sector. Nevertheless, the project managers are responsible for overall management of the construction. They are hired at the same time as the architects, attend planning and design meetings, and provide joint cost estimates with the architects. Ohio is very clear and firm that it wants the cost estimates to be realistic and accurate.

At the first indication of a possible cost overrun, we go back to the drawing board. That is, before accepting bids on the project, we prevent the overrun through redesign or value engineering. The architects and project managers work closely on the cost estimates. Each project is approved on the condition and the contingency that both architects and managers agree that the estimate is accurate and within the fixed-limit construction budget given them at the beginning of the project.

Bid competition

The project managers are also responsible for breaking bid packages into small components. By doing that, the state can achieve a number of goals. One goal of great importance is the involvement of numerous firms, which not only permits participation by many small and minority-owned businesses, but also greatly increases competition. A project's price is very dependent on the amount of competition. The small components result in active bidding by many firms, and consequently the state gets a very competitive price. Bid competition has helped tremendously in keeping to construction budgets set in 1982. It also keeps construction costs about the same as those of the federal prison system, which are much lower than the national average for state prison construction.

The project manager also takes an active role in supervision during construction. As many as seventy different firms have worked on one construction site. This has not caused problems. It is cumbersome and perhaps burdensome, but it has not caused construction delays. It has actually minimized delays and has been effective in getting the prisons built on time and on budget.

I should stress again that the corrections department in the state, which, after all, is the owner of the prison, must be clear about the budget. Two things are fixed in Ohio's projects: the budget and the number of beds. Everything else is variable, and Ohio is willing to consider any value engineering, building materials, or other cost-saving procedures necessary to stay within the budget. It is not always easy to stipulate to the contractors that they must stay on budget, and the state must continually stress that the project manager and the architects must take the construction budget seriously.

*Design
criteria*

The responsibility of the corrections department in prison construction is to make certain that the designers understand how the department will manage and operate the facility for years to come. The final design must reflect the department's management and operational philosophy and do so within cost limitations.

Ohio gives ten design criteria to the architects at the beginning of each project. The first criterion is simple: to achieve maximum interaction between staff and inmates.

Second, the state wants to reduce square footage requirements by making the utmost use of space. This condition can be met by increasing the time that spaces are used for activities. Therefore, we ask for multipurpose spaces rather than separate facilities for religious programs, meetings, and recreation. We would rather manage one single space than a lot of separate spaces.

Third, we do not build for the exception. We have an excellent staff, and we prepare them to manage incidents that can and will occur in prison. It is easy to play a "what-if" game, and ask, "How are we going to stop this?" or "What if an inmate does that?" But if the design is based on all these exceptions, the state will design itself right out of its budget. Ohio does not design for the exceptional situation.

Fourth, the state believes that people respond to their environment. If a facility is built securely, with heavy and expensive materials, it will challenge the inmates to vandalize it, and they will find some way to vandalize it. This reaction ruins the purpose of the expensive, secure environment. But if the design uses normal materials, colors, textures, and some niceties without increasing the cost, then the inmates will respond positively and not indulge in destructive behavior.

Next, we put our money into a very secure prison perimeter, but build a less expensive, more relaxed compound inside.

Sixth, we want to minimize the staff necessary for prison operation. Operational costs are the biggest part of prison costs. Ohio's expenditure for each inmate is very low, about two-thirds of the national average. That figure will not change quickly. We would like to have more money but simply cannot jump from $9,000 a year for each inmate to $15,000. Therefore, we design our prisons to minimize staff but also to improve staff efficiency.

An efficient staff is one that sees more activity, covers more space, and completes more functions.

The state minimizes future maintenance costs. Maintenance has a serious impact on the construction budget. The choice is to have cheap construction with a lot of maintenance problems in the future or relatively expensive construction with low future maintenance. Ohio puts its expenditure "up front" in construction in order to minimize maintenance costs.

Eighth, we want to keep prison systems simple. Prison staffs are not good at maintaining complicated systems, because low pay limits the number of staff trained in sophisticated, highly technical areas. The state is better off to have, for example, on-off buttons rather than computers to take care of heating, energy use, and locking systems. Furthermore, complex mechanical systems will eventually be circumvented or abused, and this problem will increase maintenance costs in the future.

Ninth, we desire to remain flexible for future expansion of existing prisons. When we build a 500-bed prison, we design it with possibilities for expansion. Each prison is designed with contingencies to build a new dormitory, expand industry, dining, and program space, and do everything necessary to accommodate the expanded bed space.

Tenth, and most important, we tell everyone to stay within the budget. We take the fixed-limit construction budgets very seriously. The state has made that criterion very clear to the architects and project managers, so they "stick to it."

Prison security

Our design focus started with a tough perimeter security. The new prisons do not have guard towers. Not only are these expensive to build and operate, but they also have proved unreliable when there is poor visibility or other problems. They are labor intensive. We have used technology—detection devices, sensors, and razor ribbon—to reduce the needs for guards. These items, also used in the federal system, have provided a very tough security perimeter. In the same way, the security envelope of each building—walls, ceilings, and floors—is very tough.

Ohio's new prisons make the utmost use of windows. Windows create a more normal environment. They give prison staff more opportunity for casual supervision of activity. Windows can be the weakest point in prison buildings, but the new prisons use unbreakable tempered glass. The prison cell windows are another innovative feature. Security windows can be expensive. Ohio designs and manufactures its own secure window grill in its prison industries. It buys inexpensive, commercial-grade glazing that can be easily opened and closed by the inmate, thus adding to the normal environment. This cell window is not a sophisticated system, and the inmates do not abuse it.

The construction of a prison with a secure perimeter and a secure envelope can be very economical because standard construction materials and techniques can be used on the interior.

Financing

Ohio is paying for new prisons through the sale of bonds by the Ohio Building Authority (OBA), the bonding agency for all state construction. The first bond issuances were sold in 1983 at a fixed rate of about 9 percent. Since then, the OBA has issued bonds at variable rates and thus taken advantage of the lower cost of borrowing. Recently, rates have been around 5 percent, and the OBA has saved up to $300,000 a month in debt-service payments.

Payments take the form of lease-rental payments by the corrections department. It gets estimates of comparable rental costs in the private sector from the state budget office. The money comes from the General Assembly in the form of state revenue funds, but there is a secondary pledge on those bonds from revenues from state penal industries.

Through these methods, Ohio has tried not only to solve its overcrowding problem but also to build 10,000 new prison beds efficiently and economically.

Analyzing the Costs of Design and Construction

RICHARD L. ENGLER

THE DECADE of the 1980s has been, and will continue to be, a period of innovation in correctional construction. Normalization of the prison environment, the use of carpeting, glass, and other "home-like" accessories, is just one, rather superficial, type of change in corrections. The field is undergoing fundamental alterations not only in architecture but in financing and operations, too. The introduction of the private sector into corrections is one more part of this revolution.

The process of designing and building a correctional institution has witnessed changes in the past few years. These changes, as in other areas of corrections, result from the extraordinary need for more cost-effective ways to address the problem of overcrowding. Many of these innovations are not really new. They are either adaptations of methods used in the private sector or refinements of previous methods of prison construction.

Two major goals of corrections today are to create confinement facilities faster and for fewer dollars. However, these pursuits should also address the value of each dollar and each hour expended. In particular, jurisdictions should examine how expended time and dollars can result in potential savings in the life-cycle costs of an institution.

Life-cycle costs

Prison life-cycle costs do not compare with anything in the private sector, where costs end and profits begin upon completion of a building.

Institutional costs do not end with the completion of a new prison facility. In fact, at that point, costs are just beginning. Operating expenses are about 90 percent of the life-cycle costs of a facility. The salaries of correctional officers are about 50 percent and another 23 percent is for civilian staff salaries. All parts of these life-cycle costs should be considered candidates for cost savings.

Richard L. Engler is executive vice-president of Hennington, Durham, and Richardson.

Prisons, unlike private rental buildings, are labor intensive. Capital costs seem to be the chief obstacle for states and counties to surmount, but construction averages only 8.7 percent of correctional construction costs in this country. Design fees account for only 0.3 percent.

The costs of poor design

On the surface, there seems to be more room for cost savings in operations than in capital costs. On a deeper level, the quality or lack of quality of design and construction can seriously affect savings, or higher expenses, in operating costs.

For example, the paybacks for energy conservation and environmental systems resulting from good design and construction are well known. Not so well known are the high expenses that result from designing a facility with inefficient staffing ratios. Consider for a moment the additional life-cycle cost for each sworn officer who is needed to compensate for poor planning, such as a system or building space that compromises security, surveillance, or supervision.

Each officer, projected over the life of the facility, will add $1 million to operating costs, at today's prices. Over the life of the institution, each operating post necessitated by inattention to design and interpretation of the program will add more than $5 million to the life-cycle cost of the facility.

Current approaches to construction

Before analyzing a recent innovation in prison construction, the collaborative design-build approach, it might be helpful to summarize some of the considerations pertaining to various other methods that are now prevalent in corrections construction. Understanding the issues will help to identify the changes and trade-offs at issue.

Today, much activity aims at creative financing and delivery through lease and lease-purchase schemes, usually for minimum-security facilities and alternative programs. Its use in low-security situations is for obvious reasons. It is easier to find sites for minimum custody facilities, especially when converting existing institutions or renovating facilities, such as college campuses. The more difficult case arises from higher-security facilities, such as maximum-security prisons and county jails.

Only a few states have developed effective private management schemes, but counties and municipal governments have shown the most interest in this approach. States have much more capacity to generate capital than counties, and they have more professional staffs to manage the process of design and construction. Counties and municipalities have a much more difficult time generating capital. So innovative financing and private management are more appealing to small jurisdictions.

The design-build approach

As noted, the design-build approach to prison construction is a recent innovation. Already used in numerous jursidictions, it usually awards a contract to a consortium of an architectural firm and a construction company. These consortia make joint bids for the design and construction job. The jurisdiction then selects the most worthy project for funding, based on both the architectural design and on cost. The design-build approach can save both time and money, since it cuts down on procurement time. Nevertheless, some jurisdictions have placed particular requirements on the process that significantly cut its utility.

Consider a hypothetical case of a correctional facility to cost $30 million. The design-build project begins by circulating a request for proposals (RFP) to contractors and developers, or to a handful of prequalified firms. The RFP may or may not include a description of required spaces, programming, and anticipated operations. The amount of information in the RFP depends on the sophistication of the jurisdiction. In some, there is no program description, much like an RFP for an office building: 5,000 square feet, heated and cooled. With a facility with such a high intensity of operations as a prison, much more information is necessary.

The intended result is similar to a simple design competition, but also includes a specific price proposal. The jurisdiction—the facility owners—can then compare designs and prices and select the one that best meets their criteria.

To prepare the proposal, the contractor teams with an architect to develop the design. If financing is also stipulated by the RFP, a financial house may also be required. However, the design-build approach is not particularly attractive to financial houses. Their success is tied directly to the success of the designer and the ability of the consortium's construction contractor to price a competitive facility. The architect must then design the project to the extent necessary for the contractor to detail and develop a responsible competitive cost proposal.

Principal issues in the design-build method

The design-build approach carries with it two important issues relating to responsibility and value. One concerns design, and the other concerns financial risk.

Architects believe that nothing should be done to compromise the interactive process that should occur between the owner (that is, the jurisdiction) and the designer. Programming and design of a typical jail or prison requires special professional expertise in all parts of the facility: zoning, operations, visiting, food service, education, and so on. Therefore, it is important that the design be thoughtfully and reflectively planned through the interaction of the architects and the owners and operators. This process will acknowledge the security and safety for those who live and work in the facility.

Underlying the design process lurks the question of value. An inappropriate design solution may look good on paper in terms of esthetics, low construction cost, or lease cost. But the capital cost is only 8.7 percent of the life-cycle cost. How will the design affect the operating costs?

The responsibility for planning and designing secure facilities is best left with specialists who understand the long-term consequences of prison design. This fact leads to the second issue of financial risk: value. Consider again the 0.3 percent of life-cycle costs—the design fee. What fees are required in the hypothetical design for a $30 million facility?

The architect must develop about 30 percent of the total design in order for the contractor to prepare a useful construction bid. Assuming an architectural fee of 5 percent of construction costs, total design costs would be $1.5 million, and 30 percent of that would be $450,000. That money is the cost to the firm of submitting its proposal.

Compare that amount with a traditional procurement in which the jurisdiction offers stipends to contenders to develop an initial design. If five firms are on the prequalified list of contenders, and the jurisdiction pays $100,000 to each, it has then already spent a total of $0.5 million. Using design-build, one firm could have completed the initial design for less than that amount, and the project would be ready for bidding.

Consider the contractor's fees. Contractors have a great deal of experience preparing bids for their work: a bid averages about 0.5 percent of project costs, or for the hypothetical $30 million project, about $150,000. The two firms in a consortium would have invested about $600,000, just for the right to bid the project. If there were five bidders, a total of $3 million would have been expended in the bidding process. If a financial house is also associated with the bid, additional bidding costs would be required.

Of course, only one of the five consortia will win. The other four will have gambled away a total of $2.4 million, a sum of money that has produced nothing.

Furthermore, the jurisdiction will still have to pay the $1.5 million in design fees for the final facility. All told, the bidders and the jurisdiction have spent a great deal of time and money, with no final result.

It is interesting to analyze what the winning bidder has to gain for the effort. Consider profits. The average architectural firm's profits are, at best, 10 percent of gross fees. That fee on the $1.5 million design contract for a $30 million facility is $150,000. Each losing architect would need to score successfully on his or her next three $30 million conventional projects just to break even for the loss incurred on this one design-build proposal. Thus, for the design bidders, there is a temptation to "shortcut" design work, thereby ignoring the jurisdiction's specific institutional needs.

It is no wonder, then, that experienced architectural firms are refusing to participate in design-build proposals and are only reluctantly participating in stipend competitions. These are, by and large, loss-inducing activities. Moreover, the question should be asked: should an owner pay for an architect's efforts to lessen risk? Probably not. The owner should select the most qualified team, pay a fair fee, and reap the benefits of an adequate planning and design process. This process will permit the utmost attention to the owner's design criteria and ensure a reasonable life-cycle operating cost, as well as an accelerated delivery of new prison beds.

Despite advantages over traditional methods, the risks of the design-build process are totally disproportionate to the perceived benefits to the designer and contractor, and the process is counterproductive to the jurisdiction.

An alternative to design-build   There is a better alternative within the design-build framework. It is an alternative that would save time, make the best use of the special talents of all team members, avoid redundancy of expenditures, and provide more cost-effective facilities—in summary, better value.

This approach requires selection of multidisciplinary teams and dedicated experts to work concurrently on the planning, design, financing, and construction of the facility. Development team members can be selected separately or as a consortium, based on their qualifications and the particular needs of the institution. The sophistication of the client's needs and resources would vary from small community to large state; therefore, the team members would also vary.

This team should include experts in financial planning, architecture, engineering, construction management, and program management. Integrating the collective resources and expertise of these different professions is essential to effective planning for the life-cycle costs of the facility. It is more productive to consider all these aspects simultaneously, rather than addressing needs analysis, physical planning, and financial planning sequentially and with no reference to one another.

This integrated team approach allows the jurisdiction to work in detail with each specialized firm and also allows the firms to work together to influence and redirect one another's progress at each phase. The proposed team approach fosters interdisciplinary communication and collaboration to enable uninterrupted development of the best solution from the start. Owners are involved at every step of the way. As the owner and architect complete the preliminary design, the program manager evaluates cost and develops a maximum price. At this point, pricing can begin through package bidding, guaranteed pricing, or total project bidding. This approach may take some realignment of procurement procedures in many jurisdictions, but none of this process is new. It has been used in the private sector for many years.

Once the concept and financing are planned, the final construction documents can be drawn up, with participation from the project manager, who can select economical materials and use practical construction schedules and techniques. The project can be bid competitively, with the knowledge that contingencies will be minimal and quality will be maximal.

The design-build project discussed earlier can jeopardize the life-cycle costs and significantly remove professional incentives and the profit incentive. But a collaborative team provides another form of the design-build method. Collaboration offers both design incentive and the potential for profit. Control and decisionmaking are key ingredients.

In summary, jurisdictions should select an appropriate planning team, coordinate the efforts of all disciplines represented on the team, keep the redundancy costs in design-build proposals to a minimum, and look for greater value through a trustworthy relationship with venders on the team.

Advantages of
Construction Management

WILLIAM J. DEASY

ALTHOUGH many capable people are working earnestly these days to reduce the rates of criminal incarceration, few professionals believe that the near term—the next five years—is going to be significantly different from the last five years. In those years, because of public opinion on drugs and personal security, judicial response to that opinion, and tough new incarceration standards, overcrowding has averaged 130 percent of rated capacity. With the growth rate of new inmates at 40,000 to 50,000 each year, the national correctional facility requirement will amount to at least $20 billion in the next five years.

Despite the billions that have already been spent, it regretfully appears that America is still in the middle of a protracted period of new correctional construction. The December 1985 issue of *Corrections Today* states that the building of correctional facilities is the tenth largest growing industry in the United States.

Reforming procurement

The construction industry can assist in easing this burden. It can add valuable insights into streamlining the procurement process. The first step is to admit that there are shortcomings in the current process. The American Bar Association's model procurement code advocates legislative reform. Eleven states have adopted that code in its entirety. Another six states have adopted it in part. Seven have enacted some form of enabling legislation to allow them to develop a more timely and cost-effective method of construction. Without question, the overwhelming weight of judicial, legislative, and professional opinion is that there should be contracting alternatives as well as the traditional method of construction.

The first important step is for legislatures to understand that professionals in the corrections industry must exercise some discretion and not be tied to a single approach to meet the diverse set of needs that exists in prison construction. Impressive savings

William J. Deasy is president and chief executive officer of the Morrison Knudsen Corporation.

35

in capital costs can result from procurement reform. New techniques can often save 25 percent on capital budgets, even on good ones prepared by architects and construction professionals. More important, new procedures can save up to 50 percent of the time required for traditional construction procedures.

However, to achieve this benefit, officials must be willing to accept the challenge of new contract relationships with the architects and contractors. The standardization of correctional facilities must be emphasized.

Traditional methods and the team approach

The traditional method of facility construction is a sequential one, with numerous political machinations. A jurisdiction retains an architect, who draws up specifications. Then the jurisdiction puts out the specifications as an RFP. Contractors prepare proposals, submit them, and go through a lengthy selection process. Finally, one is selected to build the facility.

This process is wholly workable, and it has worked for a long time. It is politically satisfying. Everyone is consulted, and if there is no time pressure and no cost restrictions, it is a fine system.

But if none of the above fit—and that is the case in most jurisdictions—the traditional method is not satisfying. It is a slow and inflexible process. It is simply not geared to today's action-oriented needs in corrections.

This problem has been confronted by the construction industry. The construction industry cost-effectiveness program is sponsored under the leadership of the Business Roundtable, which is the most prestigious organization in the construction industry. The Roundtable has viewed the creation of a team atmosphere among the project players as the most essential ingredient in cost reduction and construction control. The project team should be a group of experts, each contributing knowledge and experience to the total design and construction effort. The team should be created early in the process and be active throughout the entire process, from the conceptual planning through commissioning. The traditional process works against the team approach.

Types of contracts

What kinds of contracts and methods of construction might be recommended for construction? There are three general contract types: the negotiated general contract, the unified design-build contract, and project management.

If a jurisdiction is not able to employ one of these types of contracts, it may still be able to save time and money through alternative methods. The most common alternative method of design and construction is development of a prototype or standard facility, which may include modular construction (particularly for housing units) and prefabrication.

The negotiated general contract is a powerful tool. It is particularly useful on new construction and large reconstruction jobs that have a clear scope of work. It maintains the traditional separation between the architect and the contractor, but it advances the time of contractor selection, so that the contractor is operating with the owner during the same period in which the architect is designing the facility. That action is the most fundamental aspect of this process.

The negotiated general contract saves considerable time because it eliminates the sequential bidding and award process. In doing so, one immediately saves at least three to five months. It allows the creation of an owner-architect-contractor team. Large dollar savings result from better constructability; the general contract promotes value engineering during the design process. Value engineering is a generic term for building in cost savings in the design of the building. In the traditional process, value engineering can only be inefficiently employed through postaward change orders or other alterations to the scope of work.

Clients using this method believe the most important improvement is that they can work with a fully qualified professional corrections facility builder. Otherwise, clients may have to deal with an inexperienced builder who can, under traditional procurement, win a contract without correctional experience. In that case, a contractor is more likely both to misprice the work and misprice his abilities.

Selecting a firm

Obviously, public policy requires careful procedures to avoid abuse under the negotiated approach. Safeguards are usually created through a two-phase selection process. In the first phase, six to eight firms are prequalified, based on their demonstrated experience. In the second phase, the group is narrowed to a final group of two or three, who will then go into great detail in preparing a project proposal.

In the first phase, the six or eight firms will put forth a moderate amount of effort. In the second phase, the two or three finalists will put forth a much larger expenditure of effort. This kind of timing prevents a one-phase procurement in which a mediocre effort is made by all eight firms, who know that there is only a one-eighth chance of winning.

The negotiated general contract is the one and only contract signed for the construction. Furthermore, it can be a firm fixed-price contract, a guaranteed maximum with bonuses and penalties, or even a cost-reimbursement contract with a variable fee based on a performance evaluation. The jurisdiction can also prepackage the work and establish quotas for local subcontracts, small businesses, and minorities. A recent contract of this sort in Los Angeles came in 17.5 percent under budget.

National institute of justice

The publication by the National Institute of Justice on prison construction is an elegant testimony to the utility of these new methods (*National Directory of Corrections Construction, 1986*). It describes one hundred new jails and prisons around the country, with fascinating statistics about each construction tool, the resultant costs, and the outcome. It is eloquent in convincing jurisdictions about the advantages of alternative contracting methods. The publication gives the owner, the architect, and the engineers a wealth of information about every aspect of correctional construction.

An example of effectiveness

The three types of construction management, the negotiated general contract, unified design-build contract, and project management, are fairly new in the public institutional market, although they have been used for many years in industry, particularly for such structures as process plants. They are successful, time-tested tools. The key elements for all three are the team effort by the owner, the architect, and the builder, and the unification of responsibility and control.

The effectiveness of these techniques can best be described by an example: the use of the design-build process for a 400-bed, minimum-medium jail facility. It was constructed for the District of Columbia in Lorton, Virginia. The owner's decision to use the design-build technique was occasioned by a court order to increase capacity by a set date. The District had to do something fast.

With an architect as a consultant, the design began in March of 1986. In three weeks the contractor was excavating and developing the site. Within six months, phase one was complete; 208 minimum-security beds and areas for food preparation, multipurpose activities, and administrative functions were turned over to the owner for occupancy.

At the end of January 1987, eleven months after the original notice to proceed, phase two was complete: 192 additional medium-security beds and a single-cell maximum-security area. The entire facility was completed in less than a year.

This example demonstrated the typical effectiveness of design-build method, when there is a special need for construction and no requirement for a competitive procurement process. The technique is a powerful tool in the right situation and in the hands of professionals.

That contract also came in for $17.8 million, rather than the $20 million that was budgeted. The District of Columbia gained a facility one year ahead of schedule—an outstanding achievement for them and all the people involved.

Project management

Project management is an interesting variation on traditional methods of construction. It is a method by which a centralized manager is chosen to oversee all apsects of the construction. It is a useful alternative for jurisdictions that are uncomfortable with more innovative methods. Project management ordinarily maintains the normal degree of separation between the architect and the contractor. It is particularly useful when the scope of work is uncertain, for example, in renovations and temporary facilities. It is an excellent mechanism in situations with numerous political considerations. For example, it can be used when there is a heavy requirement for local contracting for services that are not of the highest quality, or when the architect designing the facility does not have a strong record in building correctional institutions.

In such a case, it is wise to bring in an experienced manager to handle the situation. The project manager has been used very widely in all segments of the industry. Project management is used when there is concern about cost, schedule, or the inexperience of firms that will execute the construction. It is also particularly useful in situations with serious management problems.

An owner can use the construction manager to help plan the entire range of responsibilities on multibuilding facilities or to build a single small facility. The selection of the project manager should be just as rigorous a procedure as followed to select a negotiated general contractor.

Standardization

There is no uniform rule for alternative construction methods. However, it is always important to consider standardized designs, prefabrication, and modular construction, both in structural systems and mechanical systems. The principles of standardization are simple and are based on the concept of refinement through repetition. As each building site is developed, the prototype can be further refined, and it results in greater constructability and in operational improvements. The prototype often only needs to be adapted to the specifications of the site. It saves design time. In modular construction, segments can be added or subtracted.

An important consideration in all construction is the operation and maintenance of the facility. The standardized facility offers an opportunity to apply universally standard operating procedures. Correctional officers and maintenance people can therefore transfer quickly from facility to facility. Futhermore, standardization permits a state system to use a common store of spare parts through all its facilities.

Summary

The available evidence indicates that the traditional process is not capable of procuring the construction, expansion, and renovation of correctional facilities at the accelerated pace current overcrowding demands. Contractual processes such as the negotiated general contract, design–build, and the various forms of project management I have described are needed, coupled with new construction techniques such as the use of modular units and prototypical designs. These processes allow accountability to be maintained while cost and time are substantially reduced.

The Problems of Financing Prison Construction

CHARLES B. DeWITT
and STEVEN D. BINDER

IN ALL but rare examples, modern jails and prisons are financed through borrowing. Officials recognize that cash or "pay as you go" avoid costly interest payments, but most state and local governments do not have sufficient reserves for major capital expenditures. Since most correctional institutions in the future will be built with debt financing, the critical question is, What is the best way for a government to borrow funds? Some people believe lease-purchase options, in certain circumstances, can be a useful alternative to traditional financing methods.

Lease-purchase financing is a method for buying real property through installment payments. Although technically an installment sale, lease-purchase is based on a legal arrangement in which the unit of government becomes a tenant in a facility that is nominally owned by another entity. The agreement is termed a lease because the agency does not actually receive the title to the jail or prison until all required payments are made to the entity that financed the construction. Since a lease-purchase issue is a limited obligation issued on behalf of the state or local government, income paid to investors is tax exempt in generally the same manner as a general obligation bond. Lease issues are usually termed "certificates of participation."

Similarities to traditional financing

Lease-purchase arrangements are in some ways similar to conventional financing. As an obligation of a unit of government, interest payments are not subject to federal taxation and are also generally exempt from taxes in the jurisdiction of issue. After completion of all payments, the government entity ultimately acquires title to the facility. This is usually after twenty to thirty

Charles B. DeWitt is a research fellow at the National Institute of Justice. Part of this paper is abstracted from "Ohio's New Approach to Prison and Jail Financing," National Institute of Justice, Construction Bulletin Series, November 1986.

Steven D. Binder is senior vice-president and manager of the Denver Public Finance Department, E.F. Hutton and Company.

41

years, but may be accelerated by a shorter debt retirement schedule, requiring higher payments.

Differences

The lease-purchase arrangement provides for legal ownership by another entity that leases the correctional facility to the unit of government. Many states permit creation of a public building authority for this purpose. The entity may be a public agency, nonprofit firm, or financial institution that legally owns the facility and sells the securities on the bond market. Although the corrections agency controls and operates the facility, the agency is technically a tenant. Since the leasing entity serves only as a nominal owner or "middleman," most rights and liabilities are assigned to a trustee bank.

A legislative body must appropriate funds for lease payments, and the lease agreement may be terminated by action of the government agency. This provision is termed the "nonappropriation" clause and legally qualifies the arrangement as a lease.

Since the obligation is renewable each year, the amount borrowed is usually not categorized as an ongoing legal debt and does not count against debt capacity. Like equipment rental, the facility is leased and not owned, a feature that distinguishes this method from general obligation bonds. Lease bonds are not guaranteed with the "full faith and credit" of the city, county, or state. Accordingly, they are not directly backed by the taxing power of the issuing jurisdiction, and general revenues are used to make lease payments.

Higher cost

Though lease-purchasing does offer a jurisdiction greater flexibility in financing, there are several issues inherent in the approach that state and local government must weigh.

Because the lease approach offers less safety than general obligation bonds, a higher rate of return is usually paid to the investors who purchase lease bonds with fixed rates. Depending on the security, the interest rate on lease bonds usually ranges from one-quarter to one percentage point higher than the rate paid for general obligation bonds. Since interest payments are the major expense for a government agency, fixed-rate lease bonds are almost always more expensive than similarly structured general obligation bonds of the same date of issue.

In the recent past, tax laws permitted units of government to earn interest on reserve funds. Reserve funds are established on lease bonds for several purposes, including debt service reserve (to provide funds for one year's principal and interest payments) and contingency reserve (to pay for emergencies such as damage by inmates). Depending on market conditions and prevailing interest rates, such "arbitrage" could reduce the net cost of lease-purchase bonds to a level comparable with general obligation bonds. However, the U.S. Congress has enacted legislation to prohibit this arbitrage arrangement, and interest earned on reserves may no longer exceed costs.

Repayment of debt

A key distinction between general obligation bonds and lease-purchase techniques is the difference between sources of money used to pay interest and return principal to investors. Lease-purchase methods impose a budget strain on the governmental entity comparable to conventional methods, but this procedure does not require new property taxes. Rather, general revenues are pledged, and another source of repayment must be found.

The lease-purchase method does not answer the question of how the government agency will find the funds to make the payments. Without property taxes, officials must either identify an alternative source of revenue or make an allocation from the annual budget of their jurisdiction. Thus lease-purchase offers opportunities for construction that may be otherwise impossible to finance, but lease methods are viable only when officials have identified a source of repayment for the debt.

Some states issuing lease securities for correctional facilities have developed creative new sources of revenue in place of property taxes. These include the dedication of criminal fines and forfeitures, new sales taxes, and revenues from inmate industries.

Timing

A late start on jail or prison construction can be very costly. Both rising interest rates and increased building project costs may take a toll on the project budget. Moreover, litigation on crowding may require a swift response, since construction may be ordered by a court.

A vital advantage of lease-purchase is the speed of the process. Funds can often be raised much faster than with conventional methods. How much faster depends on factors like state laws on leasing and whether an election would be required for general obligation bonds. Time savings generally range from four to eight months, and six months is quite common. This has two impacts on project costs: bid price and interest rates.

If construction costs are increasing, an early bid can save a substantial amount. Assuming a modest 5 percent rate of inflation, the cost of a $10 million project would increase at almost $42,000 a month.

During periods of rising interest rates, a delay can result in much greater interest costs. A $10 million facility would require an issue of approximately $11.3 million in securities, costing the jurisdiction about $1,151,000 per year for initial interest payments (assuming interest at 8 percent). If securities were issues at a later date when rates were just 1 percent higher, the jurisdiction would pay an additional $87,000 per year for the twenty-year duration, or a total of $1.7 million.

Variable-rate financing

Another alternative to traditional financing is the use of a variable interest rate. The state of Ohio has sold one of the nation's largest variable-rate issues and the first floating-rate securities for state correctional facilities.

In 1985 the Ohio Building Authority issued $79 million in floating-rate demand securities, backed by a lease to the Department of Rehabilitation and Correction. In contrast to traditional fixed-rate financing, Ohio's bonds bear an interest rate that changes every seven days, to follow current rates. Like a homeowner's adjustable-rate mortgage, Ohio securities pay interest that is raised or lowered according to changes in the economy. During the year following issuance in April 1985, the rate paid to investors moved down to 4.5 percent, up to 9.0 percent, and back down to 4.8 percent. During that year, the state saved more than $3 million by issuing variable-rate securities.

The Ohio bonds bear a lower rate because the interest rate is fixed for a very short period of time. Since the rates change weekly, they do not offer the protection that their rate will remain at the level set on the date of issue. This protection warrants a premium, which is why government agencies must pay more to lock in a fixed rate. Likewise, for investors, the Ohio bonds offer a high degree of financial liquidity, since they may be redeemed with only one week's notice. Termed the "demand" feature, this arrangement permits Ohio to pay a much lower interest rate than would be required for conventional fixed-rate bonds.

Risks of variable rates

The short-term variable-rate feature that results in reduced interest rates also creates a degree of risk that does not accompany conventional methods. Interest rates will vary and may not remain at the level in effect at the time of issuance. If rates increased, it would not be long before savings initially realized by variable-rate securities would be offset by higher interest payments.

Although low interest rates are possible because investors maintain the prerogative to "demand" their money, this procedure represents a significant risk to a unit of government issuing variable-rate securities. Someone must guarantee the cash to investors, since the government has already spent the money on building the new correctional institution. This guarantee is known as a "letter of credit" and represents the guarantee by a financial institution that funds will be provided for investors who have cashed in their bonds.

Should investors exercise the demand feature, the funds must also be borrowed from a financial institution to return their principal until the securities can be resold. An underwriter is retained to remarket the securities that are "put back" by investors, and the risk of this procedure is that market conditions might make it difficult or impossible to sell the securities in a timely fashion. Both the letter of credit and the remarketing fees represent additional costs associated with the demand feature of variable-rate securities. These costs have the effect of reducing the savings from variable-rate securities.

Precautions   Periods of interest rate volatility offer considerable risks to jurisdictions using variable-rate financing. Large rate increases can wipe out any savings resulting from the variable feature. However, there are precautions that can be taken as safeguards. The primary protection against dramatic increases in interest rates is a feature called conversion, which permits the jurisdiction to change from variable to fixed interest rates at any time. Using this feature, some agencies have issued variable-rate securities in anticipation of a drop in rates. When a lower interest rate becomes available, an agency may exercise the conversion feature to lock in a reduced rate for the remainder of the term.

As a final measure of safety, Ohio has provided that the entire issue may be redeemed or repurchased by the state in the event that the building authority wishes to arrange for a new financing package.

Options in financing   Because financing alternatives now available to state and local officials are numerous and diverse, general conclusions about financing decisions are inappropriate. Each city, county, and state should consider the unique factors that bear on its ability to raise capital and repay debt.

Evaluation of financing options has become a complex undertaking. Mistakes can be costly. Officials should exercise caution when considering alternative finance methods. A variety of strategies for borrowing may be considered by officials planning to build correctional institutions, and positive or negative consequences of their financing decisions may endure for as many decades as the institution itself.

Lease-purchase financing can be a viable alternative for agencies that are blocked from use of conventional methods. However, lease bonds are likely to cost a governmental entity more money, in the form of higher interest payments.

Variable-rate securities can cost less than both fixed-rate lease bonds and general obligation bonds, but this approach presents certain risks that must be carefully considered.

Political
problems

These alternatives and options seemingly leave a jurisdiction with numerous problems in financing new institutions. However, in a very real sense, there are no real financing problems in the construction of prisons and jails. There are only political problems.

From the mid-1970s to the early 1980s, private financing firms began a serious effort to work with communities to solve legal financing problems in jurisdictions that were under court order for overcrowding and had no legal mechanism for bond financing. This was not an attempt to "privatize" corrections or to offer the communities a full-service "turnkey" facility including private management. It was rather an uncomplicated attempt to introduce the notion that communities could lease a facility without entering into a debt and do so in a cost-effective manner. In large measure, this attempt did solve the financing problems of many jurisdictions.

What it did not solve was the political problem, or, at least, the education problem. The lease-purchase financing technique evolved over a period of nearly ten years. The ability to get the financial community to accept risky, year-to-year, long-term leases has been far easier than explaining to state and local politicians how their political decisions affect financing and construction.

In the course of the evolution of lease-purchasing, some states developed the concept of the turnkey "design-build" package for the construction of their prisons. With the notable exception of the state of Missouri, this concept has failed. It is not cost effective for an architect to bid on one of these projects, and states do not get the best product, qualitatively or financially, from the design-build process. But unfortunately, some jurisdictions are no longer concerned with getting the best product, but only a completed product. This is another indication of the need to address the political problem and not the financing problem.

The prison as public improvement

The problem for prison and jail construction is the failure of the political process to recognize that prisons are the most unpopular of public improvements. Politicians must confront that fact. Once it is confronted, the financing, construction, and outfitting of the facility can be addressed.

The American people are intolerant of crime. This has been demonstrated by the doubling of the incarceration rate in the United States over the past fifteen years. But at the same time, the public is not ready to "pick up the tab" for this crackdown on crime.

The innovative idea of lease-purchase financing tries to solve this structural problem. It permits jurisdictions to avoid a confrontation with the political problem of going to the voters for permission to build. The turnkey package approach, which is in effect the finance-design-build model, requires something more. In it, the jurisdiction does not separate construction from financing. As a result, a contractor who would do a much better construction job than its competition can still lose the bid because the competition may join with a design firm or financial house that can do a better job in that area.

Instead of bidding the facility by component and getting the best job in each area, the political expediency is for the jurisdiction to keep a distant relationship and simply occupy the facility after it is built. This puts all the risk on the private firms involved in the project. Even when they design and build it exactly to the jurisdiction's specifications, the jurisdiction can still decide not to occupy or not to make lease payments. Thus the jurisdiction can tell its constituents—the voters—that it is not really spending any more money on prisons than in the past.

But that is simply not true. The jurisdiction is spending more. And it is this problem of politics or education that is the real one in prison financing.

Lease-purchase and the voters

There is another aspect of the political problem that should be addressed, namely, the damage to our democratic institutions that results from lease-purchasing through the avoidance of a public vote on prison construction. In actuality, this is neither an issue nor a constitutional concern. When properly structured, a lease-purchase agreement is not a debt. It has true "walk-away" provisions. There is a history of state supreme court cases in several jurisdictions that indicate that if the jurisdiction wishes to abandon a lease-purchased facility, it can do so without liability for damages. In each lease-purchase agreement, investors, bond rating agencies, and investment bankers are concerned about the possibility of the jurisdiction withdrawing from the lease.

The issue of the public vote on issues of indebtedness usually has to do with property taxes. The notion is that if a general obligation bond is issued, and those bonds can be paid by taxes on voters' property, then the voter should have a voice in that indebtedness. A lease-purchase agreement is not a general obligation. Jurisdictions have walked away from leases in the past. Furthermore, there will probably be instances in the next fifteen years of more walk-aways resulting from overbuilding of prisons, which lease-purchasing may cause in some jurisdictions.

"Getting around the voters"

A more subtle aspect of this problem is what might be termed the moral issue of "getting around the voters." But this issue is also overblown. Every state executive or county commissioner who must make a decision about correctional construction is mandated through state statutes and often the state constitution to provide adequate jail and prison facilities. To the extent that the executive or commissioner does not provide adequate facilities, he or she is breaking the law.

If a state or local official has the duty to provide certain facilities but cannot do so because the electorate will not vote for a bond, then where does the blame lie? Clearly, it lies in the same structural problem mentioned above. That problem—the political and educational problem—must be confronted in a realistic way.

Private Industry and the Future of Corrections

EUGENE C. THOMAS

THE AMERICAN Bar Association has taken the view that privatization should be approached in a deliberate way, with the full awareness of all the issues implicit in the privatization of American prisons and jails. The association is not questioning the use of private industry in the contracting of certain traditional functions, such as facility design and construction, and services such as the provision of food and medical and psychiatric care. However, the general management and operations of an institution and the private ownership of its physical plant remain delicate issues. These cannot be discussed in a vacuum. Privatization of corrections can affect every area of U.S. society, and it is prudent to consider what those effects might be, before committing the correctional system to this new course.

Fortunately, there is already a large body of knowledge and experience, not only from the correctional system, but also from other segments of the economy, which can be brought to bear on the debate over privatization. Financial institutions, health care facilities, and Medicare nursing home care all have aspects that are applicable to the current needs in corrections.

The correctional world is now made up of two groups. On one side are firms of the private sector, who look at the issue of private construction to determine if they have a role, and if so, what that role is. On the other side is the public sector, consisting of elected officials, government appointees, and agencies, who are trying to define the role of the private sector and decide whether to delegate their responsibilities to it.

Legal constraints

Both sides should recognize that, in a legal sense, current laws and regulations regarding privatization should not be seen as constraints on future activity. The government can do anything it wants about privatization. Though various regulations and

Eugene C. Thomas is president of the American Bar Association and chairman of the board of the Boise law firm of Moffatt, Thomas, Barrett & Blanton.

legislation on limits to private enterprise exist in many jurisdictions, experience has shown that these rules can be amended or circumvented if the responsible leaders make an effort to do so.

The American Bar Association (ABA) view—that privatization must be approached deliberately—is one that is probably supported by everyone in the field of corrections. To assist in implementing this policy, the ABA is developing model contracts, enabling legislation, and other documentation for jurisdictions interested in considering private involvement in some aspect of their correctional system.

Capital for corrections

Despite wide agreement on this policy, there are other aspects of private enterprise in corrections that all persons in responsible positions should consider. First, in this era, there is severe competition for public funds. Public funds are a finite resource. Corrections competes for those funds with highways, schools, health care, and various other public needs and services. It must also compete against movements like Proposition 13 in California, and the Gramm-Rudman legislation at the federal level, which aim at lowering the total amount of public funds available. There will come a time in government when there is simply no more money, and the bills will not be paid if the jurisdiction has not stayed within rigid fiscal guidelines.

The issue, then, becomes how to attract private funds and capital to corrections. Clearly, private funds can be obtained if the enterprise can be structured in such a way as to make the investment good for business. If it will not permit business to generate a profit, no private operator will go into a correctional enterprise. Private involvement in corrections must make sense for the investor, or the investor will not enter.

Changes in the tax laws are also important to the private sector. For example, when lease-purchase arrangements first appeared, tax shelter treatment was available for any leased correctional facility. Because of recent changes in the tax laws, those tax investment credits no longer exist. So a private owner of a facility may not have any particular advantage over the public operator; it is more difficult now for a private operator to be cost-effective in competition.

On the other hand, if the burden of expense is shifted from public to private, the private sector is also going to pay sales taxes, income taxes, and property taxes, further reducing the relative cost-effectiveness of the private sector.

Politics in corrections

But these economic issues cannot be considered in a vacuum. The decision about privatization still concerns, in essence, a system of justice. The public will expect corrections to deal with the people who are populating these institutions: Who are they? What can be done about their alcohol and drug addiction? Their poverty, illiteracy, and unemployment? What can be done to prevent their criminal behavior? What does the public expect of these people when they are released?

These questions must be considered by both sides before a contract can be signed. Today, everyone in corrections is very troubled because the current answer to these questions is "not much." Because of overcrowding, managers of institutions cannot manage; they can only warehouse people. If that situation persists, notwithstanding privatization, how will the private sector stand the heat of public criticism of warehousing human beings?

Privatization in other fields

The corrections system must learn from the experience of hospitals. Hospitals contracted with private nursing homes for patients needing continuous care. However, the cost of operation was greater than the funding really permitted. As a result, the private nursing home contractors had to return to the hospitals to renegotiate contracts, owing to higher-than-expected operation costs.

The law has tended to look at similar situations favorably and has granted relief when an operator has not been given a fair compensation level for a return on equity. The same relief would apply if the contractor finds, after the contract is signed, that he must meet standards of performance that were not clearly specified in the initial agreement. In corrections, both sides must anticipate that the business of managing public responsibilities is a very demanding one.

Any company interested in corrections or other public service must be a strong corporate entity, with a strong capital structure and strong management. Nothing could be worse for corrections than the employment of firms that cannot do the job:

Democracy and corrections

The final issue for private firms in corrections might be termed "democracy in action." Every American is an expert on who gets locked up. Every American is, and should be, an expert on human liberty. Therefore, it is not surprising that, in a democratic society, the public always has the right to change government policies, particularly those concerning the treatment of citizens. In the long run, incarceration rates and sentencing lengths will vary widely.

As a result, private prisons will be faced with changes in population, which may affect their profit margin. The private sector must expect radical changes in public attitudes, expectations, and demands for correctional policy.

The American people have arrived at a point of gross disenchantment with law, justice, and corrections—especially prisons. A typical wisecrack in public meetings is, "If he wasn't a crook when you sent him to prison, don't worry; he will be when he gets out." The disenchantment results from the lack of safety on the streets and even in the home. The public is going to demand results from prison programs. If citizens do not get results, namely public safety, they are going to exercise their democratic right and spend their money on highways and schools rather than on ineffective prisons.

So any use of the private sector is fraught with political, economic, and legal difficulties. There is no easy answer about the use of private firms in corrections. In the short run, the most sensible answer would be to test the ideas about private sector participation and see if corrections can attract responsible companies with sufficient capital and good management. There is plenty of room for testing and experimentation.

In the interests of liberty and justice—for both law-abiding citizens and for prison inmates—correctional professionals must study the issue thoroughly or else run the risk of public disenchantment.

One aspect of the issue of prison construction that must be stressed is the issue of freedom. Incarceration is, after all, a situation in which Americans are deprived of their liberty for cause, in connection with criminal behavior. Americans who are managing that deprivation of liberty must accomplish the act legally, humanely, and effectively. How can this be accomplished in the years ahead? What is the nature of the "road ahead" for corrections in America?

The goal of a safe society

From a legal perspective, several aspects of American society will influence the course of corrections policy. First, the American people will demand a safe society. There was a blush of embarrassment recently when some Russian emigrés returned by their own choice to the Soviet Union. Some said that their reason for leaving America was the crime they encountered in the streets of this land, even in broad daylight. Americans would like to brush this aside as propaganda, but they, too, are dissatisfied by the level of crime in American streets and the overall state of lawlessness in American society.

Because Americans resent taxation and resist and test it at every turn, they demand that corrections cost the least amount possible. People do not like criminals. It is not easy for a taxpayer or a legislator to allocate money to the criminal program when citizens view it as benefiting the violator of the law, in preference, perhaps, to education, transportation, or indeed, the victims of crime.

So American corrections policy will be based on the need to promote a safer society while keeping financial investment in the corrections system as low as possible.

An increased role for jails

The crisis we are facing in corrections will probably be moved "upstream" in the correctional system: from the prisons to the jails. It is in jail that the offender usually has his first encounter with the system. This encounter may be as a petty offender, or as a youngster, or simply as a person awaiting indictment, trial, and sentencing for a first offense.

What happens in the city and county jails, therefore, should be an area of far greater emphasis than it is today. The public as a whole has a dawning awareness of this fact. If early offenders can be identified and a criminal career prevented, society will be better able to reduce crime.

American society must change its patterns of behavior. There is no reason to finish third, behind Soviet Russia and South Africa, in imprisoned people per capita.

If we focus on jails in the effort to improve the system, a key area for improvement is in jail management. It is an embarrassment to the United States that in most counties the elected sheriffs are still using patronage to fill jail management positions. That system is one hundred years out of date.

The quality of jail facilities must be upgraded by modernizing the laws to permit proper treatment of hardened criminals. The same hardened criminals now in prison had formerly come through the jails, and they obviously were not treated correctly there. That is to say, they were not classified correctly. As a result, our children and our neighbors may have been placed in danger by letting a criminal on the streets who should have been in prison. That system is counterproductive to justice in America.

Consolidation

Consolidation of facilities in the interest of efficiency and effectiveness should be another goal for corrections. Facilities should be clustered in order to permit the best kind of services for the young males who are predominant in the prison population. Consolidation can also help to address the drug and alcohol problems of that group.

Facilities for these young offenders—particularly jails and other "entrant" facilities—should accomplish what, obviously, was not accomplished in the schools before these youngsters found their way into the corrections system. Jails should deal with illiteracy. By the time offenders get to prison, education programs are usually too late to be effective. The intensive professional effort should be at the beginning of an offender's career. By waiting until the person becomes an inmate of a prison, the warden has to deal with an individual who has already been through the hands of the police, sheriffs, and county jails many times.

So the road ahead will bring a significant change in jail management because the public will demand it, if not because of wisdom, then because people are penurious, and the present system is a waste of money.

Legislation and privatization

Constitutional test cases will have to be run through the state courts, because every state has its own constitution and every state will try to capture the benefits of private participation in prison construction. Too many states have constitutional and statutory prohibitions that stand between the public and the benefits that result from private enterprise. Those matters have been addressed by constitutional amendment in some states and by statutory amendments in almost all states. It is ridiculous not to bring those benefits to corrections. But it will still require test cases in order to verify to the satisfaction of the financial community that new laws will stand the test when money is committed.

Taxes and privatization

The public agencies engaging in criminal justice activities should be able to employ the private sector to improve operations. Many experts believe that privatization is quicker, better, and cheaper, yet privatization is prohibited in many jurisdictions. There is no reason why, in the future, the law should not be changed to make the operation of public agencies quicker, better, and cheaper.

On the other hand, the private organizations wishing to become involved in corrections should be able to enjoy the same benefits of tax-free operation that the public agencies now enjoy. Why tax a private operation that is running a jail or prison? No sheriff or prison warden in the country now has to pay taxes to run the same jail or prison. One would not add extra weight to a race horse that one wants to win. Similarly, additional tax burdens should not be placed on a private enterprise that is being asked to perform a public function. Without the additional tax burden, we could get a clear indication of the extent of savings resulting from privatization. If privatization is a worthy goal, society should encourage it and find ways to give it a clear chance to succeed. This goal may require facility authority bonding, municipal-exempt treatment of rent, or other mechanisms that remove unequal treatment to private financing and construction.

Parole and probation

The road ahead also leads to a renewed emphasis on intense probation and parole, despite the current federal policy of restricting probation. America is going to have to extend a hand to people whom it wants to lead away from criminal life styles.

In this regard, the United States has a great deal to learn from the Soviet Union. The Russians have a strong sense of community, and when a person returns from prison there, they try to help that individual succeed because that is the mark of the success of their criminal justice system.

Parole and probation are the ways in which the "public hand" can reach out. Because it costs so much when incarceration fails to rehabilitate, the American people eventually will see the wisdom of these policies.

Finally, there will be a change in correctional philosophy in this country, a moving away from the current "hard line" against crime. Although the road ahead may be tortuous, the American correctional system is going to become more and more like its hospital system: we now hospitalize people only if absolutely necessary, and only for the briefest time possible, in order to control costs. Eventually, society will have to answer the questions, "Can we safely give offenders a shorter length of stay?" and "Can we safely cut the cost of their length of stay?" Resolving these questions may help the country to achieve its goal of a safe and just society.

Overcrowding and justice

Let me conclude with a personal reference to a very old, dear friend of mine, who was a warden in a penitentiary in the western United States. His was an old, archaic facility. It was nothing to be proud of, and it was overcrowded. But he was a good man and a sincere, straightforward person.

Each inmate who came to his prison was brought to the warden's desk. There he told them, "This joint has everybody in it that we have room for. It is overcrowded, so you are coming in, and somebody is going out. One of these days you will have been here awhile, and you will be the guy who wants out. I will be the guy who decides if you go or not. So keep your nose clean, and that is the way we are going to get along here." Then the man was marched out.

This friend of mine would often tell this story, and invariably, he would end it by saying, "Isn't that a hell of a way to run an institution? Isn't that a hell of a note for justice in this country?" I agreed with him then; I agree with him now.

Conference Participants

Benjamin Baer
U.S. Parole Commission

Steven D. Binder
Senior Vice-President, E. F. Hutton and Company

Samuel J. Brakel
Research Attorney, American Bar Foundation

Arnold Burns
U.S. Deputy Attorney General, Department of Justice

Norman A. Carlson
Director, Federal Bureau of Prisons

William D. Catoe
*Deputy Commissioner for Operations, South Carolina
Department of Corrections*

Warren I. Cikins
Brookings Institution

Helen G. Corrothers
Commissioner, U.S. Sentencing Commission

Lois-Ellin Datta
*Associate Director, Program Evaluation and Methodology Division,
General Accounting Office*

H. E. Davis, Jr.
Purchasing Agent, County of Los Angeles

William J. Deasy
President and Chief Executive Officer, Morrison Knudsen Corporation

Thomas J. Dever
Chief, Correctional Services, Fairfax County Sheriff's Department

Charles B. DeWitt
Research Fellow, National Institute of Justice

Joseph diGenova
U.S. Attorney for the District of Columbia

Roger V. Endell
Commissioner, Department of Corrections, Alaska

Richard L. Engler
Executive Vice-President, Henningson, Durham, and Richardson

Donald R. Erickson
*Manager, National Criminal Justice Program,
Morrison-Knudsen Company, Inc.*

Gerald M. Farkas
Assistant Director, Federal Bureau of Prisons

Arthur F. Foren III
Justice Design Manager, Ehrenkrantz Group & Eckstut

Gerard Frey
*Planning Coordinator, Missouri Department of Corrections
and Human Services*

A. Lee Fritschler
Brookings Institution

Mary Galey
Project Manager, Federal Bureau of Prisons

Roberto J. Gambach
Architect, Gambach Architects, Inc.

Kerry Hayes
Vice-President, Planning and Development, Pride, Inc.

Craig Higgins
Office of Senator Mark O. Hatfield

Scott Higgins
Chief of Facilities Development, Federal Bureau of Prisons

William L. Hood
Vice-President, Continental Illinois National Bank

Wade B. Houk
Assistant Director for Administration, Federal Bureau of Prisons

James M. Ingram
Senior Vice-President, Leo A. Daly Inc.

Gary King
Vice-President, E. F. Hutton & Company

Larry King
CAO Project Manager, Criminal Justice
County of San Diego

Gert Koerner
Vice-President, Morse Diesel, Inc.

Jack K. Lemley
Senior Vice-President, Morrison-Knudsen Company, Inc.

James Lenertz
Operations Manager, Morrison-Knudsen Company, Inc.

Robert Love
Director for Administration, Orange County General Services Agency

Robert Maloney
Manager, Design Services, Morrison-Knudsen Company, Inc.

John W. McCluskey
*Chief Deputy Director for Corrections, Virginia State
Department of Corrections*

Bill McCollum
U.S. Representative, Republican of Florida

Walter M. McKew
Business Development Manager, Morrison-Knudsen Company, Inc.

Patrick H. Molloy
Attorney, Barnett & Alagia

Donald Murray
*Legislative Representative for Justice and Public Safety,
National Association of Counties*

Edward W. Murray
Director, Virginia State Department of Corrections

Edward K. Norton
Assistant Vice-President, Morse Diesel, Inc.

Frank Panarisi
Director, Deloitte Haskins & Sells

Jerome N. Pasichow
*Assistant Commissioner, Capital Planning, New York City
Department of Corrections*

William J. Raczko
*Deputy Assistant Commissioner, New York City
Department of General Services*

Alfred S. Regnery
Partner, Leighton & Regnery

Walter Ridley
Associate Director, District of Columbia Department of Corrections

Ira Robbins
Professor of Law, American University

Laurie Robinson
Director, American Bar Association Section of Criminal Justice

James C. Rushing III
President, Detention Development Corporation

Richard P. Seiter
Director, Ohio Department of Rehabilitation and Corrections

Donn Smith
Manager, Project Finance, Morrison-Knudsen Corporation

John L. Smith
Attorney, Barnett & Alagia

Chris Steinman
Deloitte Haskins & Sells

James K. Stewart
Director, National Institute of Justice

Eugene C. Thomas
President, American Bar Association, and Chairman,
Moffatt, Thomas, Barrett & Blanton

Anthony Travisono
Executive Director, American Corrections Association

Joyce Van Dyke
Consultant, National Institute of Justice

Richard J. Ward
Corrections Specialist, U.S. Department of the Navy

Bradford P. Wilson
Research Associate to the Chief Justice of the Supreme Court
of the United States

Shirley A. Wilson
Director, Office of Criminal Justice, Government of the District of Columbia

John Yoder
John Yoder & Associates

John L. Zalusky
Economist, American Federation of Labor and Congress of Industrial
Organizations